Bach's
Choral Music

Unlocking the Masters Series, No. 20

Bach's
Choral Music
A Listener's Guide

Gordon Jones

𝄞

AMADEUS
PRESS

An Imprint of Hal Leonard Corporation
New York

Published in 2009 by Amadeus Press
An Imprint of Hal Leonard Corporation
7777 West Bluemound Road
Milwaukee, WI 53213

Trade Book Division Editorial Offices
19 West 21ˢᵗ Street, New York, NY 10010

Printed in the United States of America

Book design by Snow Creative Services

Library of Congress Cataloging-in-Publication Data

Jones, Gordon, 1946–
  Bach's choral music : a listener's guide / Gordon Jones.
    p. cm. —— (Unlocking the masters ; no. 20)
  Includes bibliographical references.
  ISBN 978-1-57467-180-3 (alk. paper)
  1. Bach, Johann Sebastian, 1685–1750. Cantatas. 2. Bach, Johann Sebastian, 1685–1750. Oratorios. 3. Bach, Johann Sebastian, 1685–1750. Masses, BWV 232, B minor. 4. Cantatas—History and criticism. 5. Oratorio. I. Title.
  ML410.B13J65 2009
  782.2'4092—dc22

                                                                          2009037625

ISBN 978-1-57467-180-3

www.amadeuspress.com

To members of the Putney School in Putney, Vermont—

past, present, and to come

Contents

Preface   ix

Chapter 1. Bach's Life and Times   1

Chapter 2. What Is a Cantata?   15

Chapter 3. Thirty Selected Cantatas, First Group   25

Chapter 4. Thirty Selected Cantatas, Second Group   45

Chapter 5. Thirty Selected Cantatas, Third Group   57

Chapter 6. *St. John Passion*   71

Chapter 7. *St. Matthew Passion*   91

Chapter 8. Mass in B Minor   117

Chapter 9. Other Works: Motets, *Ascension Oratorio*,
   Magnificat, Christmas Oratorio   133

Further Reading   137

Glossary   139

CD Track Listing   157

Preface

This book is intended to demystify the choral music of J. S. Bach, to help those who already enjoy his music to listen to it with greater inwardness, and to encourage those who would like to know how to talk about this music to understand it better. We cannot really see a flower until we know its name.

Above all, however, my hope is that through reading this book and listening to the examples of Bach's work on the enclosed CD, some may venture to take part in performances of his music.

Listening to this music has never been easier. Everything Bach wrote has been recorded many times. The cantatas, for example, exist in complete or nearly complete sets conducted by Nikolaus Harnoncourt, Helmut Rilling, Ton Koopman, and John Eliot Gardiner, to name just a few, and all of these performances are wonderful in different ways. We can acquire Bach's music on CD or purchase and download it via the Internet; we can even use online resources and vendors to sample the music in advance to check tempo, style, sound. And then with one click we can have Bach pour into our computers wherever we are in the world.

It is a little harder to hear this music live; it takes a little effort. But it is performed all over the world, in cities, towns, colleges, churches, and schools. In December, one is never far from a performance of the *Christmas Oratorio*; many of us will have a choice of performances of the passions during Holy Week; and the B Minor Mass is now commonly heard.

Harder still, but entirely feasible for all, is to perform this music. Community choruses abound everywhere, and in them people are singing both for their own pleasure and for the delight of others. At times in Bach's life—at Weimar, for instance—he had access to performers of the very highest order. But he spent most of his working life, twenty-seven of his sixty-five years, in Leipzig, where he really did have to work with amateur musicians. He raided the town band for people to play those trumpet and horn obbligatos, and where the likes of the composer Jean-Baptiste Lully had *Les vingt-quatre violons du roi* (The King's Twenty-four Strings), Bach had his *Schenkenvirtuosen*, best translated as "beer fiddlers."

We know that Bach tailored his music to the forces available, and we know he was willing to drum the notes into recalcitrant schoolboys, full-throated grocers, and even members of his own family, in order to produce music that was so much greater than the sum of its parts. I recall a time when, living in Botswana, Africa, I discovered that two accomplished oboists and a brilliant violinist lived in the town, as well as a capable soprano and baritone. "Wachet auf!" I said (referring to one of Bach's chorale cantatas). The orchestra as a whole was enthusiastic and rose wonderfully to the challenge. Sixty people, who for the most part had never sung in a choir before, learned the tricky opening chorus, with its fast-moving fugue.

I hope that my readers will stumble across similar opportunities, and if they do, I also hope they will remember the words of Henry Van Dyck: "Use what talents you possess: the woods would be very silent if no birds sang there except those that sang best."

I have had the opportunity to try out some of my ideas on a number of colleagues and students at the Putney School in Vermont, a progressive boarding school with an unrivaled arts program, whose musicians are particularly blessed by singing and playing in a music department rehearsal room whose centerpiece—if one discounts three harpsichords, a clavichord, a matched set of viols, and a Bösendorfer piano—is a complete run of the *Neue Bach-Ausgabe*, a bequest from the late, talented Peter Gram Swing, a lover of the school who taught at Tanglewood for many years, who led the music program at Swarthmore College, and who was also a close confidant of P. D. Q. Bach. My first thanks therefore go to him. I regret never having met him but have had good talks with those who knew him well.

Many Putney people have listened to my Ancient Mariner ramblings about the Bach cantatas. Some who have been of great assistance are Greg Brown, former music director at Putney and a countertenor of considerable talent; James Wallace, Putney's present music director and a classy performer of Bach's organ works; Brian Cohen, printmaker and quite a *Schenkenvirtuoso*, or beer fiddler, himself; Christopher Lehmann-Haupt, keen-eared listener and polymath, who reminded me to pay tribute to the camels we hear loping along in BWV 65, *Sie werden aus Saba alle kommen* (They Will All Come Forth Out of Sheba); and Abijah Reed, mathematical wrangler, merry wag, accomplished and accurate singer, and maker of more than one harpsichord, who has supplied me with replacement strings at extremely short notice on more than one occasion and has always been ready to commiserate with me while I am tuning.

I wish also to record fond memories of my two favorite former keyboard teachers, both no longer with us: the harpsichordist Edith Starbuck of Portland, Oregon, who was apt to say, "Bach will never ask us to do something that can't be done, so stop making such a meal of it," and "If it's stepwise it's legato, if it's skipwise it's detached, whatever Glenn Gould might decide to the contrary"; and Douglas Steele of Manchester, England, who taught me to play continuo from the figured bass, to read scores by gumming paper over the piano reduction, and to take down Bach chorales from hearing him play them, when I was about fourteen years old. Douglas would insist that I be prepared to transpose any one of the forty-eight preludes and fugues in *The Well-Tempered Clavier* to another key of his choosing and to leave out a voice line from a fugue and sing it instead. After he once told me that in some circles it was not considered polite to allow leading notes to fall to the fifth at a perfect cadence, when I asked, "Why not? Bach did," he replied, "Lord, now lettest thou thy servant depart in peace." It was a little mystifying at the time.

Bach's
Choral Music

Bach's Life and Times

For Western music, 1685 was a good year, an *annus mirabilis*. George Frideric Handel was born in Halle (Prussia); Domenico Scarlatti, the son of his highly musical father, Alessandro, was born in Naples; and in Eisenach, Johann Sebastian Bach joined the ranks of the perennially musical Bach family. All three men were also able performers, and as composers they were extremely prolific. Handel produced 42 operas; 29 oratorios, including the well-known *Messiah*; more than 120 cantatas; and many orchestral and instrumental works. Scarlatti is famous to this day, notably among keyboard students for his 555 keyboard sonatas, or *essercisi* as he called them. But in terms of the number of compositions and their scope and complexity, Bach had the most fertile musical imagination ever, and his methodical and productive efforts were legendary in his own time and remain so today.

One thinks of Mozart, who wrote operas, symphonies, sonatas, chamber pieces, songs, and even a Requiem in D Minor, which he may have believed was intended for himself, it having been commissioned by a mysterious visitor from beyond the grave, as he thought. Or of Wagner, whose fourteen operas have a running time of almost fifty hours. But for sheer quantity, range, and invention, J. S. Bach wins the prize, as a look at the BWV catalog instantly shows. The *Bach-Werke-Verzeichnis*, published in 1950, is organized thematically, rather than chronologically. BWV 1–224 are cantatas; BWV 225–49 are the large-scale choral works; BWV 250–524 are chorales and sacred songs. Many of these first 524 items are the subject of the present work. The remainder (BWV 525–1126) comprise organ and keyboard music, pieces for lute, chamber music, orchestral music, and a number of canons and fugues for unspecified performers.

We are well provided with materials for the study of Bach's life and the age in which he lived. The 1873 biography by Philipp Spitta, still in print, remains very readable and gives us an especially useful account of Bach's musical forebears, as does the *New Grove Dictionary of Music and Musicians*, now available online. But the touchstone is Christoph Wolff's *Johann Sebastian Bach: The Learned Musician* (2000). Wolff also (in 1998) revised and enlarged David and Mendel's *New Bach Reader* (NBR). First published in 1966, this entertaining and useful work gives us Bach's life as told through contemporary letters and documents. One might expect such a book to be a little dry, but instead it fascinates and entertains. For instance, we read that early in his time as court musician at Arnstadt, Bach was rebuked by the consistory of the church where he played the organ, for confusing the congregation during the chorales with "many curious *variationes* in the chorale, and mingl[ing] many strange tones in it . . . or even play[ing] a *tonus contrarius*." If we look back from the perspective of Bach's many elaborate and decorative chorale preludes, we may perhaps see the beginning of something very distinctive in the incident. Apparently the church authorities did not see it that way. In the same meeting he was also rebuked for paying visits to the wine cellar during the sermons. Six months later he was again in trouble, for introducing a "frembde Jungfer"—an unfamiliar maiden—into the choir loft (Wolff 1998, 47–48).

A little later, in 1705, Bach was in trouble once more:

> Johann Sebastian Bach, organist here at the New Church, appeared and stated that, as he walked home yesterday, fairly late [at] night . . . six students were sitting on the "Langenstein" (Long Stone), and as he passed the town hall, the student Geyersbach went after him with a stick, calling him to account: Why had he [Bach] made abusive remarks about him? He [Bach] answered that he had made no abusive remarks about him, and that no one could prove it, for he had gone his way very quietly. Geyersbach retorted that while he [Bach] might not have maligned him, he had maligned his bassoon at some time, and whoever insulted his belongings insulted

him as well . . . [Geyersbach] had at once struck out at him. Since he had not been prepared for this, he had been about to draw his dagger, but Geyersbach had fallen into his arms, and the two of them tumbled about until the rest of the students . . . had rushed toward them and separated them. (NBR, 43)

The *New Bach Reader* offers us much insight into Bach's career, but we do not get an inward portrait of Bach's thinking from his own hand. He complained a fair amount about money and benefits, about getting his due recognition; at one point he wrote a grumpy letter to a friend who had sent him a gift of wine, because he had had to pay excise duty on it. But we do not find any record of his emotional or intellectual life.

What was it that made this great mind tick? It was the love of God, apparently; every cantata, and many other of his works, was inscribed "SDG," which stood for *Soli Deo gloria*—"To the glory of God alone," one of the five *solas*, or basic tenets of the Protestant Reformation, intended to distinguish it from Roman Catholicism.

The Thirty Years' War and its aftermath

For Bach and other people of his time, the love of God was by no means an uncontroversial matter—as it hardly ever is. For thirty years, from 1618 to 1648, most of the powers of Europe were fighting on German territory, the theme being the conflict between Protestants and Catholics, the undertheme being the quest for political control of Europe. No war is pretty, but the Thirty Years' War was unusually savage. Fought largely by mercenaries, it resulted in the environmental degradation of huge areas of Germany; great population loss through slaughter, famine, and disease; and economic chaos for the participating powers. Though it was formally resolved at the Treaty of Münster, enmity continued for quite some time afterward.

The German states lost perhaps 20 percent of their overall population and, most significantly, about 40 percent of males. They also lost, according to some estimates, more than two thousand castles and about twenty thousand towns and villages, largely to Swedish forces, which contributed to a strand of hatred in the German consciousness that continues today.

One important consequence of the war and the uneasy peace that followed was the decentralization of power. The modern term for this is *balkanization*—the division of a basically homogeneous region into many smaller territories, each of which had sovereignty, in both political and religious matters.

One such state was the Free State of Thuringia, which emphatically endorsed the Lutheran Reformation, and in one of the chief towns of Thuringia—Eisenach, where Marin Luther had himself lived as a child—Bach was born.

Bach's early years

Johann Sebastian Bach was the youngest child of Johann Ambrosius Bach, one of a huge family of musicians. Christoph Wolff tells the family's story in *The New Grove Bach Family* (1983). Bach's father was an organist at St. George's Church and taught his son to play the violin and keyboard instruments. Part of an organist's job was to get organs to work and keep them working. J. S. Bach in due course was a major figure in organ construction and maintenance, and one can only suppose he spent many hours as a child hanging out around, and probably inside, organs. Was he pressed into working the bellows? More than likely. Most of Bach's uncles were professional musicians also, and one of them is believed to have taught him to play the organ.

Bach was the first in a tradition of historians of his own family: circa 1735 he began to compile a genealogy of the family, which can be found in the NBR.

Bach himself may not have been fully appreciated as a budding musician by his own newly acquired stepmother; when his father died in 1694, in response to an inquiry as to whether the family could bring forth another Bach to take the dead Johann Ambrosius's place, she is reported to have said, "God has caused the springs of musical talent in the Bach family to run dry within the last few years."

Bach, aged ten, went on to receive a first-class musical education, for he moved in with his eldest brother, Johann Christoph Bach, who at twenty-three was already the organist of St. Michael's Church in Ohrdruf, not far from Eisenach. We may surmise that Johann Sebastian's musical experience with his brother was quite varied. We know that one of the two organs for which his brother was responsible was in a sorry state and required a good deal of work to keep it playable. Probably, J. S. Bach busied himself at this task alongside his brother. Besides his musical education, he also thrived at the local school, not least in his Latin studies.

When he was fourteen, Bach and his friend Georg Erdemann won choral scholarships to St. Michael's School in Lüneburg, near Hamburg, a long journey of about two hundred miles to the north that the boys are thought to have walked large portions of. Besides singing in the choir, Bach may have played the monastery-school's three-manual organ. During his two years there, he also continued with his general education and no doubt came into contact with the sons of many highly placed individuals in Northern Germany, for the school was highly competitive.

While in Lüneburg, Bach would have visited Johanniskirche (the Church of St. John) and heard (and possibly played) the church's famous organ, built in 1549. The Böhm organ, so named after Georg Böhm, its most famous master, can be heard today in the same church or in online video clips. It is a massive machine, and one would like to hear Bach's mighty Toccata and Fugue in D Minor (BWV 565) played on it. There is evidence that Bach studied with Böhm, and C. P. E. Bach stated that his father loved and studied Böhm's works. The great organist Jan Adams (Johann Adam) Reinken was also nearby, in Hamburg, and Bach visited him frequently. Through such contacts, Bach got to know the work of the great Dietrich Buxtehude of Lübeck, whom he later visited (in 1705), walking the 250 miles each way.

After he graduated from school, Bach's musical career had a somewhat bumpy start. He returned to Thuringia (likely to Ohrdruf) and from there obtained a town-organist post in Sangerhausen, about seventy miles to the north. But before he could take it up, the post was given to someone who had more influence with the local duke than did Bach. A few months later, at the start of 1703, he entered the service of the duke of Saxe-Weimar. He later described his position as *Hoff Musicus* ("court musician"), but the court payroll has him as a "lackey"—work involving the performance of valet services and odd jobs. He did not stay long. In August of that year he was engaged as organist of the New Church (also known as St. Boniface's Church) in Arnstadt. He had earlier inspected the new organ at this church and gave the inaugural recital on it. Throughout his life, Bach did a rather brisk trade in organ inspection, which involved auditing the work of organ builders, recommending repairs, and not infrequently helping the builders receive what was due to them. Wolff tables twenty-one such engagements, throughout Bach's life, from age eighteen until two years before his death.

The new appointment took Bach about 110 miles to the southwest of Weimar but landed him only 10 miles from his birthplace. At Arnstadt his duties were not particularly demanding, and he was quite well paid. Best of all, he had a fantastic new organ, which was tuned to a newly developed system that permitted a relatively wide range of keys to be used. Bach was preoccupied all his life with the question of temperament: How may one modify "pure" tuning, based on perfect fourths and fifths, which can be used to construct one scale in perfect tune, so as to permit one to wander off into other keys without generating the effect of sourness? Bach's contributions to this debate were many, but none more decisive than his famous "Forty-eight," the two sets of twenty-four preludes and fugues that constitute Books 1 and 2 of *The Well-Tempered Clavier (Das wohltemperierte Clavier)*. These musical pieces cycle through each of the major and minor keys, and as a set they are playable only if one tunes in the system known as *equal temperament*. So the new organ at the New Church must have been a delight.

Bach had composed organ music during the Ohrdruf years; many of the so-called Neumeister Collection of choral preludes date from pre-1700. At Arnstadt he began composing organ music quite seriously—music not yet really contrapuntal, but more in the North German manner of florid, quasi-improvisatory preludes, in the style of Buxtehude. Though Bach had not exhausted what Buxtehude had to teach, and indeed had not yet met the great man of Lübeck, we may hear that he was already drawn to the tight control of motif, whereby a terse musical idea is explored over and over. This approach is evident in one of his earliest and yet most popular works, the Toccata and Fugue in D Minor (BWV 565), which no one who has attended a Halloween party or watched Disney's *Fantasia* can fail to have heard—it has even found its way into the cell-phone ringtone repertoire. This work dates from the Arnstadt period and may have begun its life as an improvisation. Throughout his career, Bach wrote many pieces that had the flavor of improvisation, music that sounds as if the performer is thinking it up as he or she goes along. The C Major Prelude in Book 1 and the F Major Prelude in Book 2 of *The Well-Tempered Clavier* are good examples of this improvisatory sound.

As already noted, the authorities at the New Church tried to keep the brilliant young man in check, but on and off, matters were tense. He decorated the chorales in outlandish fashion; he had a way of visiting the wine cellar during the sermons; he invited a strange young woman into the choir loft. For his part, Bach was apparently dissatisfied with the standard of the choristers, and he let people know it.

More serious was his unauthorized absence from his post for quite some time in 1705–6, when he walked the 250 miles from Lübeck to Arnstadt, to visit Dietrich Buxtehude. This journey must have taken almost ten days on the way out, and perhaps longer on the way back. He stayed with Buxtehude several months more than planned.

There is a story that both Bach and Handel wished to become amanuenses (studio assistants) of Buxtehude but that each man drew the line at marrying the old fellow's daughter, which appears to have been a condition.

And there was the falling-out with the student Geyersbach, already discussed.

Mühlhausen

By 1706, it was time for Bach time to move on, perhaps from the family milieu, but certainly from the New Church. He gained a more lucrative post as organist at St. Blasius's Church in Mühlhausen. Pay and living conditions were better, and a good choir was available. Moreover, marriage was now an option. Four months after arriving in Mühlhausen, Bach married his second cousin, Maria Barbara Bach of Arnstadt. They had seven children, four of whom lived on and two of whom themselves became important—Wilhelm Friedemann Bach and Carl Philipp Emanuel Bach.

In Mühlhausen, Bach began to write cantatas and to be more interested in vocal than in organ music. From this time we have what is probably his first cantata, BWV 150, *Nach dir, Herr, verlanget mich* (Lord, I Long for You). If one compares this cantata to what Buxtehude and others were writing at the time, it is clear that only a new and distinctly different talent could have written such an impressive work. Despite a tiny orchestration (two violins, bassoon, and continuo), the music covers a huge range. It features dramatic tempo and character changes; the chorus "Leite mich" (movement 4) has strange, startling shifts of mood. The second has a most extraordinary viola da gamba obbligato. The cantata ends with a mighty chaconne (movement 7), which so impressed the later composer Johannes Brahms that he worked it into his Fourth Symphony.

More striking still, however, was the cantata (which he called a "Congratulatory Church Motet") that Bach wrote in 1708 for the inauguration of the city council at which the newly elected burgomasters (town councilors) were installed. His audience must have been astonished by BWV 71, *Gott ist mein König* (God Is My King), which is scored for seven separate vocal and instrumental ensembles. The instrumental and vocal "choirs" comprise three trumpets and timpani; a string ensemble; two oboes and a bassoon; two recorders and a cello; a continuo section led by the organ; a solo vocal quartet; and a four-part ripieno chorus. The cantata has seven movements, the first and last of which feature the full ensemble—a dramatic noise indeed. There are other surprises, too, including an alto aria accompanied by the trumpets and drums, as well as the continuo team. It is quite a struggle for the alto soloist to hold his (or her) own. Unusually for Bach, the cantata was published, as were other Mühlhausen-period vocal works. However,

BWV 71 is the only one of these to have survived. No post-Mühlhausen vocal works were published.

Three weeks after the first two performances of BWV 71, the church and town officials voted to approve the renovation of the organ in St. Blasius's Church, to Bach's design. His specification called for a new thirty-two-foot stop on the pedals. This means that the largest pipe of the rank is thirty-two feet long rather than the standard eight feet, which sounds the notes as written. A sixteen-foot pipe sounds one octave lower than written, and the thirty-two sounds two octaves lower than written. Also on the pedals was a set of chimes (called *glockenspiel*), which the parishioners particularly desired. There was also a whole new third manual, or keyboard, with new pipes throughout.

Given his successes and the town's enthusiasm, it is surprising that Bach was not at Mühlhausen long. After less than a year, he became organist and concertmaster back in Weimar. He had certainly been humiliated there earlier on, but now the thought of working with a group of highly able musicians must have been appealing. He had already expressed a little vexation at the amateurish nature of music making in Mühlhausen when in June the call came to give the inaugural recital on the newly renovated organ in the castle church at Weimar. The incumbent, Johann Effler, was thought not to be up to the task. Bach played; Effler decided it was time to retire; the duke concurred. Bach was offered the post at a handsome salary, and Effler was allowed to retire at his full salary. Money alone would probably have done the trick, but Bach must also have been attracted by the position of "chamber musician and court organist," which meant that he would be performing exclusively with professional musicians. He departed Mühlhausen on good terms and returned there to make some guest appearances, presenting two more election cantatas (now lost) and continuing to assist with the organ-rebuilding plan. As late as 1735, when his son Johann Gottfried Bernhard Bach was appointed organist at St. Mary's Church in Mühlhausen, the elder Bach went along and examined the newly rebuilt organ without charge, even noting what portions were still missing.

Weimar

Bach and his family moved into an apartment just a few minutes' walk from the ducal palace. Not long after, their first child, Catharina Dorothea, was born. Also born at Weimar were Bach's two most significantly musical children, Wilhelm Friedemann and Carl Philipp Emanuel.

Understandably enough, in Weimar Bach devoted a great deal of his energy to the production of instrumental music, and initially he was influenced by Italian music such as that of Vivaldi, Corelli, and Torelli. He made arrangements of Vivaldi concertos for organ and harpsichord, and from the Italians he learned the excitement of driving rhythms and bold harmonies. Of particular importance was the *concerto grosso* form, in which solo players (concertino) and full orchestra (ripieno) alternate. The "Brandenburg" concertos represent the flowering of this genre.

Bach's production of fugues began in earnest in Weimar. He had the opportunity to play and compose for the organ and to perform a varied repertoire of concert music with the duke's ensemble. BWV 846–69 and BWV 870–93, the two books of *The Well-Tempered Clavier*, were published in 1722 and 1744, but they represent material assembled by Bach throughout his life, and much of it dates from the Weimar period. He also began work on his *Orgelbuchlein* (BWV 599–644), or *Little Organ Book*, a collection of chorale preludes, elaborate harmonizations, and fugal fantasies based on Lutheran chorales. This development of chorales was a fundamental aspect of his art as a choral composer, the flowering of which was to come during his Leipzig period (1723 onward). He did compose cantatas while in Weimar, including some of his very finest, especially in the obbligato writing, for he had the best instrumentalists at his disposal. BWV 21, *Ich hatte viel Bekümmernis* (I Had Much Heartache), is one example. Another Weimar cantata that continues to be a great favorite is BWV 147, *Herz und Mund und Tat und Leben* (Heart and Mouth and Deed and Life), the cheerful opening chorus of which is on the enclosed CD; BWV 147 also features what is perhaps Bach's most famous piece, the chorale fantasy now known as "Jesu, Joy of Man's Desiring."

No one quite knows why, but relations between Bach and the court at Weimar deteriorated dramatically at the end of his time there. He was put in jail for a month, supposedly for having pressed too hard to secure his dismissal from his post.

Cöthen

Once out of jail, Bach found work as Kapellmeister with Prince Leopold of Anhalt-Cöthen. Leopold was himself a musician and appreciated Bach highly. He gave the composer considerable latitude and paid him well. However, the prince was Calvinist and did not favor the use of elaborate music in his chapel. In consequence, most of Bach's music at this time was instrumental and orchestral. While at Cöthen he wrote the suites for orchestra, the cello suites, and the solo violin music. Because of the circumstances, little of Bach's work from this period was sacred choral music.

One moment in Bach's time at Cöthen stands out, and for the worst of reasons. In July 1720, Bach returned from a trip and was met on the outskirts of town with the news that his wife Barbara had died, leaving Bach with considerable family responsibilities. He and his first wife had had seven children together. But it was not long before he married again—to Anna Magdalena Wilcke, for whom he wrote the *Notebook for Anna Magdalena Bach*, inscribed in her own handwriting as *Clavier-Büchlein vor Anna Magdalena Bachin, Anno 1722*, a book of carefully selected keyboard pieces brought together to help her learn to play the keyboard. Even today, beginning piano students learn the collection's Menuet in G Major. It is one of the first pieces we play in which the hands have to move in opposite directions. Unfortunately, about half the book has disappeared, depriving us of some insight into Johann and Anna's musical relationship. She was much younger than her new husband (by seventeen years). Together they had another thirteen babies. Anna Magdalena was a brilliant soprano soloist. She had been a little involved in the music making at Cöthen. She may have been the soloist in one of Bach's most brilliant solo cantatas, BWV 51, *Jauchzet Gott in allen Landen* (Praise God in Every Land), first performed in

Leipzig in 1730. The final movement of this cantata, setting the single word *Alleluia*, is one of the tracks on our CD.

Leipzig

Bach later said that he had intended to spend the rest of his life at Cöthen; yet in 1722 he applied for the dual position of cantor at St. Thomas's Church in Leipzig and music director of the city of Leipzig, and after some hiccups and false starts in the interview and application process, he was appointed, on April 22, 1723. He had presented several compositions for his interview and audition in February, one of which, BWV 23, *Du wahrer Gott und Davids Sohn* (You True God and Son of David), was one of his finest. The other, BWV 22, was a rather more frilly affair. It seems Bach tried to provide something for everyone.

The position was a complex one. He was cantor of the Thomasschule, a school adjacent to St. Thomas's Lutheran Church in Leipzig, as well as director of music in the principal churches in the town. This was essentially a government post; at last he was through with having to work for the aristocracy. In Leipzig he was responsible principally for church music, which he had had a taste of in Mühlhausen, but now he was operating on a larger scale. On the other hand, he was once again limited by the fundamentally amateur nature of this endeavor. He was also thrust into political machinations, the chief features of which were the antics of two groups, a monarchist faction (to whom Bach owed his appointment) and a city–state faction. The price exacted by the latter for agreeing to Bach's appointment was control of the school, and in particular control over Bach's working conditions. The basic problem was that Bach and his champions regarded him as the leader of church music in the city, whereas the city faction was more concerned with the running of the school. There were constant squabbles about money right through Bach's time in Leipzig, as we may read in the *New Bach Reader* (Wolff 1998). He had to teach the students of the Thomasschule to sing, as well as provide music for services at the two main churches in Leipzig, St. Thomas's and St. Nicholas's. His contract required him to teach Latin, but he was allowed to subcontract this work—and did.

The first decade in Leipzig was dominated by the cantata. We do not know quite how many cantatas he wrote, though it seems he may have composed five annual cantata cycles in his first six years. Many have been lost, but we do now have about two hundred of them. The cantatas' creation involved more than pure music composition, of course. Every cantata required finding or developing a text, which had to be appropriate to the liturgical material, usually drawn from the Gospel stories selected for the week in question. Some cantatas were based solely on Lutheran hymns; others involved working with a librettist. All that settled, the work had to be composed (usually written out in fair copy—no rough drafts or notebook entries for Bach). The parts would then have to be copied, and though he did have some assistance in this, there is evidence that he examined and copied all parts. Next came teaching soloists their parts, working with instrumental obbligato players, rehearsing and performing the whole thing, and then packing it away and starting on the next one. He did this one after another, week by week, one cantata at a time. One may surmise that he sometimes miscalculated—overestimated—the abilities of his players, and then there would be some backing and filling. He did not have many permanent players, perhaps only eight, and would have had to beg, borrow, and steal the rest of the required players from the university and the town—the so-called beer fiddlers. Singers, too, had to be found. The school provided the sopranos and altos, but tenors and basses were recruited in the town.

Cantatas represented the bulk of Bach's work, but there were other significant works also, not least the huge oratorios, the two passions BWV 244 and BWV 245 (the *St. Matthew Passion* and the *St. John Passion*, respectively). In 1729 he broadened his reach by taking over as director of the Leipzig Collegium Musicum, a group featuring the best professional musicians in town. The group performed twice a week for two hours in Zimmerman's Coffee House, where Bach produced his *Coffee Cantata* (BWV 211) in 1732. He produced a great deal of instrumental music in the last years of his life, much of it performed in Zimmerman's.

In 1733 Bach presented the first two movements of his Mass in B Minor to the elector of Saxony in the vain hope that he would be appointed court composer, perhaps as part of a plan to gain more influence in Leipzig. He went on to add the other mass sections, partly by reworking material from some of his more successful cantata movements. The Mass was probably never performed as a whole in his lifetime, but it is certainly one of his greatest works. It is frequently performed now and has been recorded many times.

The great works of his later years—*The Musical Offering* (BWV 1079) and *The Art of the Fugue* (BWV 1080)—were instrumental and, in the case of the latter, even abstract. Those who come to love Bach by working with this book will certainly want to get to know *The Art of the Fugue*, written in four voices (all within singable range) but without words. It can be performed on the piano, harpsichord, or organ; it has also been recorded, in whole or in part, by the brilliant viol ensemble Fretwork; by brass ensembles; by the Pittsburgh Symphony Brass; by the Emerson String Quartet; and even by banjoist Béla Fleck, bassist Edgar Meyer, and friends.

Less well known is *The Musical Offering*, written as a challenge to a theme supplied by King Frederick II of Prussia.

By 1749 Bach was quite sick and became blind. It is thought that he was diabetic. We know little about his last days, other than that his last composition was to dictate the revisions to a chorale prelude to his son-in-law. He died on July 28, 1750, moderately wealthy, and besides the sum of 1,159 Thalers (the equivalent of three years' salary), he left seven harpsichords and ten stringed instruments of various kinds.

But the most important detail of his end is not known. We do know that his funeral took place three days later. We know that the hearse and church fees were waived for the service. But sadly, we do not know what the music was.

What Is a Cantata?

The meaning of the word *cantata*, simply enough, is "something sung." It is of Italian origin and came into use in the sixteenth century. The singers are usually accompanied by instruments, and always so in the case of Bach's cantatas. Bach did write a set of unaccompanied (a cappella) cantata-like pieces, which he termed *motets*. BWV 225, *Singet dem Herrn ein neues Lied* (Sing to the Lord a New Song), and BWV 226, *Jesu, meine Freude* (Jesu, My Joy), are well-known examples of these. Bach's cantatas almost always have several separate movements.

For the most part, his cantatas were sacred in nature. He did write a number of secular cantatas, of which about thirty-five are extant. These include the famous *Coffee Canata*, a wedding cantata, a serenade, and even a hunting cantata. But most cantatas had a liturgical role within the church service. The cantatas are usually based on an ancient German chorale or hymn tune. In a few cases, the text of the cantata is wholly supplied by the chorale; more usually, however, there will be a combination of chorale, scripture, and original meditative texts supplied by a number of brilliant librettists. Though Bach was often asked by his employers not to make his cantatas too theatrical, they are usually quite dramatic in form, resembling small oratorios.

It is astonishing that Bach found time to write so many cantatas. Thirty cantatas have been selected for detailed attention here, choices based in part on some of their variations of structure, or because they display Bach's technique and musical purposes particularly clearly, but mainly because they show him at his very best. The reader will likely come across live performances of many of the works chosen and might even be lucky enough to participate in performances of some of them. It would be hard to find a college choral society or community or church chorus that does not have one or more Bach cantatas in its repertoire. Remember that Bach's choral music, especially that of the magnificent Leipzig years, was "community" music, and despite the abundance of outstanding recordings now available, it is as community music that the cantatas are still best understood and experienced today.

There are two hundred or so extant church cantatas, though it seems that a great many have also been lost. For several periods in Leipzig, Bach was bringing a new cantata forward for performance approximately weekly. As described in the previous chapter, this would likely involve his giving thought to the content of the Holy Gospel for the Sunday in question, collaborating with a librettist, realistically assessing the musical forces available to him, composing the music (usually written out in manuscript fair copy), copying parts (he did have some assistance here, but the evidence is that he did much of it himself), checking the parts against the score, teaching individual soloists and instrumental players the more difficult material, rehearsing the whole work, and then performing it.

Let us not forget that he did also have twenty children, several of whom required and got a first-class musical education from their father. Legend has it that Bach was not able to settle in to formal composition until he went up the stairs to his composing room at about 9:00 p.m., a bottle of brandy tucked under his arm.

Liturgical and other contexts

The bulk of Bach's choral music was intended for use within church services. In most cases he knew exactly what occasion he was writing for, and the near-comprehensive series of cantatas for the ecclesiastical year shows how focused and consistent his thinking was. He did parody earlier works to find material suitable for a later, clearer conception of purpose, and he did reuse material written for specific dates in the Leipzig church year for other purposes. (The word *parody* does not connote ridicule in this context.) He was a consummate self-borrower.

Some choral works were religious in character without having a church purpose. Some think that the great solo cantata BWV 51, *Jauchzet Gott in allen Landen* (Praise God in Every Land), may have been written for performance outside the context of the church; the reasoning here is that since the vocal line is too demanding for a boy soprano, it could not have been used in church. No one knows.

From about 1739 onward, Bach increasingly wrote, organized, and collected his music for purposes other than the Leipzig churches' needs. Thus we see some secular choral music (and a lot of instrumental music). Nonetheless, it makes good sense to view his choral music as inseparably bound to the needs of the church.

The chorale

Chorale is the term used to describe a hymn in the Lutheran church, to be sung by the entire congregation. Martin Luther's insistence that church services should be conducted in German, not in Latin, led to a need for hymns and other works in the vernacular. Chorales tend to have simple and singable tunes, because they were originally meant to be sung by the congregation rather than by the choir. The choir would be seen as a part of the congregation and would lead in the singing. Luther composed some chorales himself, including "Ein' feste Burg ist unser Gott" (A Mighty Fortress Is Our God), which Bach used for BWV 80, the "Reformation" cantata. For other chorales Luther used older tunes, including Gregorian chants, and provided new text. Such is the case with "Christ lag in Todesbanden" (Christ Lay in the Bands of Death), the basis of BWV 4.

Many of these chorales were harmonized by Bach; he seldom wrote original chorales. His chorales were collected by Riemenschneider in the *Neue Bach-Ausgabe* and are available in a number of reasonably priced books even today. Students of composition frequently, even constantly, use them for study. Many people other than musical specialists also know them well. We hear them all the time around us, as well as in church.

Bach wrote many chorale fantasias; "Jesu, Joy of Man's Desiring" is a famous example. It is found in Cantata 147 (BWV 147.6 and BWV 147.10) and can be heard on our CD. (The designation BWV 147.6, as with similar catalog numbers, stands for BWV 147, movement 6.) He also wrote many chorale preludes for organ.

Bach's librettos

Concerning the librettos of Bach's cantatas, James Day, in his 1961 book *The Literary Background of Bach's Cantatas*, made an interesting attempt to "correlate baroque elements in the texts of Bach's cantatas with baroque elements in the music." Readers are recommended to look at this useful and interesting book, the year-2000 edition of which is still in print. It is well known that more than one of Bach's employers asked him to avoid theatrical elements in his sacred music. We also know that Bach did not always cooperate with this request. The opening da capo aria of BWV 81, *Jesus schläft, was soll ich hoffen?* (Jesus Sleeps, What Hope Is There for Me?), contains an uproarious storm scene, which Jesus quells in the B section with the aid of the ever self-contained oboe d'amore, only to be undermined in turn by the musical inevitability of the da capo aria, which insists on taking us back into the midst of the storm! On the whole, Bach did avoid the sensational theatricals, but his setting of words, or rather, their underlying ideas, is always dramatic, in the sense that he always endeavored to re-create the concreteness and immediacy of the thoughts under consideration. Day (2000, 25) puts it beautifully:

> Quite often, Bach appears to have aimed at a dramatic effect—but not in the sense that Handel or Mozart employed music dramatically; his idea of drama, as we shall see, corresponded much more closely to that of the German baroque dramatists, being rhetorical and sententious, working on the plane of ideas rather than that of personalities.

This restrained approach to dramatics is usually the case with Bach, though not always. When in the *St. John Passion* (BWV 245) the veil of the temple is "riven in twain, from the top to the bottom," and the earth shakes, we have musical effects that would pass for operatic. The *St. Matthew Passion* (BWV 244) has several highly theatrical moments, such as the recitative immediately following the death of Jesus, in which are described the thunder and lighting, the earthquakes, and the graves' vomiting forth their dead.

There are several types of libretto. Perhaps the simplest is that which confines itself to verses from the Bible, without adding any new material. The "Wedding" cantata, *Der Herr denket an uns* (The Lord Cares for Us), BWV 196, is a case in point. Bach simply took four verses from Psalm 115. Other cantatas set verses from old chorales. BWV 4 is an especially notable example of this method. Possibly Bach found himself in a quandary following the death of a favorite librettist and had to take the most expedient course. BWV 100, *Was Gott tut, das ist wohlgetan* (What God Does Is Done Well), sets all nine verses of the chorale *Innsbruck*. More often than not, however, Bach combined scripture passage with the work of librettists. The collaboration between Bach and his librettists was often close. BWV 244, the *St. Matthew Passion*, is a clear example. His librettist Picander conceived of the idea of a dialogue between the children of Zion and God's faithful on Earth, and this notion led Bach directly to the idea of writing for double choir.

Current live performances of the cantatas

Obviously enough, the mother church of modern Bach Cantata performance must be St. Thomas's in Leipzig, where the motets are performed on Fridays and the cantatas are frequently performed on Sunday evenings. St Thomas's was where the twenty-year-old Mendelssohn revived the *St. Matthew Passion* in 1829, after the seventy years' silence that fell following Bach's death. Several U.S. cities are blessed with organizations devoted to the systematic performance of Bach's cantatas. Boston, for example, has Emmanuel Music, based in Emmanuel Episcopal Church. Emmanuel Music, founded in 1970 with the goal of performing all the Bach cantatas in their liturgical setting, has performed the entire cycle twice, and the work continues. In addition,

Emmanuel Music has performed the Mass in B Minor, both passions, and much else besides.

Holy Trinity Lutheran church in New York hosts a similar endeavor. Bach Vespers Choir and Orchestra is a professional ensemble that performs regularly at Holy Trinity and also tours. On a more modest but equally appealing scale, every city and town in the world, it seems, has one or more amateur community choirs, and most of these perform Bach from time to time. For more information on Web sites that publish information on upcoming performances of the cantatas, scores of the cantatas themselves, and information on the specific venues mentioned here, please refer to the Further Reading section in the back of the book.

Recordings

Many complete or near-complete recordings of the cantatas are available. Helmut Rilling, currently music director of the Oregon Bach Festival, recorded all of the cantatas between 1969 and 1985; a wonderful complete set also was produced by Nikolaus Harnoncourt and Gustav Leonhardt. Ton Koopman, with the Amsterdam Baroque Orchestra and Choir, has done them all. Recently, Masaaki Suzuki and Bach Collegium Japan have completed their recording of virtually the whole of the sacred choral music.

Thirty selected cantatas

It has been a pleasure to listen to the whole collection of Bach's sacred cantatas, three times: in the outstanding complete recording put together over the years by Nikolaus Harnoncourt and Gustav Leonhardt, and in Helmut Rilling's performances; but Bach Collegium Japan have won my heart. This is the ensemble whose work I use all the time in talks, and for this book.

It is always useful to make comparisons. Readers will be able to sample these performances in a variety of ways. Of course you can get a general feeling by browsing online, where listening to second extracts will enable you to check out tempos, the "flavor" of the singer and instrumentalists, and the music itself. If you wish to gather together a comprehensive selection, or a complete set, of the cantatas, you would probably do well to select one performer; otherwise, duplications will result. The Harnoncourt/Leonhardt series follows the BWV numberings and is available as a magnificent boxed set of sixty discs, and all of these can be purchased for digital download, as well. The Rilling, Bach Collegium Japan, and other sets follow their own somewhat idiosyncratic groupings.

I have selected thirty of the greatest cantatas for detailed comment. My choice is based in part on the quality of the music—an absurd notion, admittedly, since every cantata contains something of interest. If these pages described only the cantatas I have omitted from my selection, we would still be considering the work of one of the world's greatest musical geniuses. I have also chosen works that demonstrate some of the more important salient stylistic features. But principally, my aim in making the selection has been to tempt my readers to explore further, both in their listening and by way of getting practically involved in performance. I will try to help readers imagine what it might have been like to be among Bach's first listeners, but I have also given some thought to how listeners might have felt when rediscovering Bach in the age of Mendelssohn. I have also intentionally chosen some music that is quite startling, such as BWV 5, *Wo soll ich fliehen hin?* (Where Shall I Flee?), in which the devil gets to play the trumpet.

Some readers may object to some of my omissions. That is fine; if you do, it means you have already started on the process of exploration and probably know the works you might wish to champion far better than I do. And I do object to some of my own omissions; to get the number down to thirty, I had to make the choice to leave out BWV 192, *Nun danket alle Gott* (Now Thank We All Our God), which is based on perhaps the most famous chorale of all. Again, I decided to keep down to a few the selection of choruses in D major and featuring trumpets and drums. Dozens of these movements exist, all of them wonderful and worth listening to, given world enough and time. One recommendation for further exploration would be the solo cantatas. There are several of these, including the great alto cantatas BWV 54, *Widerstehe doch der Sünde* (Keep Away from Sin), and BWV 170, *Vergnügte Ruh, beliebte Seelenlust* (Contented Rest, Beloved Soul's Desire). These cantatas were recorded by the legendary countertenor Alfred Deller, and modern performances by Andreas Scholl and by the great Japanese countertenor Yoshikazu Mera are worth exploring, as is a recording of BWV 170.1 by Angelika Kirchschlager.

Bach cantatas: Selected list

Here, then, is the selection of thirty of Bach's church cantatas, listed by BWV number. They will be discussed in three groups of ten, in the following three chapters.

BWV 1   *Wie schön leuchtet der Morgenstern* (How Brightly Shines the Morning Star)

BWV 5   *Wo soll ich fliehen hin?* (Where Shall I Flee?)

BWV 9   *Es ist das Heil uns kommen her* (Our Salvation Has Come to Us)

BWV 20   *O Ewigkeit, du Donnerwort* [II] (O Eternity, You Thunderword)

BWV 21   *Ich hatte viel Bekümmernis* (I Had Much Heartache)

BWV 23   *Du wahrer Gott und Davids Sohn* (You True God and Son of David)

BWV 34   *O ewiges Feuer, o Ursprung der Liebe* (O Eternal fire, O Source of Love)

BWV 36   *Schwingt freudich euch empor* (Soar Joyfully Upward)

BWV 39   *Brich dem Hungrigen dein Brot* (Break Your Bread for the Hungry)

BWV 41   *Jesu, nun sei gepreiset* (Jesus Now Be Praised)

BWV 42   *Am Abend aber desselbigen Sabbats* (On the Evening, However, of the Same Sabbath)

BWV 51   *Jauchzet Gott in allen Landen* (Praise God in Every Land)

BWV 56   *Ich will den Kreutzstab gerne tragen* (I Will Gladly Carry the Cross)

BWV 60   *O Ewigkeit, du Donnerwort* [I] (O Eternity, You Thunderword)

BWV 63 *Christen, ätzet diesen Tag* (Christians, Etch This Day in Metal and Marble)

BWV 65 *Sie werden aus Saba alle kommen* (They Will All Come Forth Out of Sheba)

BWV 66 *Erfreut euch, ihr Herzen* (Rejoice, You Hearts)

BWV 67 *Halt im Gedächtnis Jesum Christ* (Keep Jesus Christ in Mind)

BWV 75 *Die Elenden sollen essen* (The Wretched Shall Eat)

BWV 76 *Die Himmel erzählen die Ehre Gottes* (The Heavens Declare the Glory of God)

BWV 83 *Erfreute Zeit im neuen Bunde* (Joyful Time in the New Covenant)

BWV 96 *Herr Christ, der einge Gottessohn* (Lord Christ, Only Son of God)

BWV 97 *In allen meinen Taten* (In All My Actions)

BWV 100 *Was Gott tut, das ist wohlgetan* (What God Does Is Well Done)

BWV 104 *Du Hirte Israel, höre* (You Shepherd of Israel, Hear)

BWV 105 *Herr, gehe nicht ins Gericht mit deinem Knecht* (Lord, Do Not Pass Judgment on Your Servant)

BWV 140 *Wachet auf, ruft uns die Stimme* (Awake, Calls the Voice to Us)

BWV 147 *Herz und Mund und Tat und Leben* (Heart and Mouth and Deed and Life)

BWV 158 *Der Friede sei mit dir* (Peace Be with You)

BWV 180 *Schmücke dich, o liebe Seele* (Adorn Yourself, O Dear Soul)

Thirty Selected Cantatas, First Group

F inding recordings of the Bach cantatas is dangerously easy using the Internet and credit cards. Most people seem to settle upon one ensemble for preference, or two or three.

Having more than one recording of something one is interested in is useful if one wishes to delve into matters of interpretation, such as tempo and phrasing. It can be sometimes disconcerting to listen to performances side by side if the performers have selected different tunings. A440 (meaning that the tone A above middle C has 440 cycles, or beats, per second) is the standard concert pitch now, though one can also discern variants. For example, I have heard it said that there is something called "Boston pitch," reported to be at A444, a pitch that apparently is also favored also in Europe. Studies of instruments in museums show that pitch in the seventeenth century may have been as low as A373. Standard "baroque pitch" is by consensus now A415, though some harpsichordists who play French music favor A392. The organ in St. Jerome's Church in Vienna is at A457. The 1714 organ in Strasbourg Cathedral was A391. In 1711 the inventor of the tuning fork favored A423.5. In 1936 the American Standards Association settled on A440.

I do recommend acquiring scores of everything you listen to. Downloadable scores of Bach's cantatas are available from a number of Web sites. The *Bach Gesellschaft Ausgabe* (BGA) edition of the complete works of Bach, publication of which began in 1851 at the hands of Moritz Hauptmann and others, varies somewhat in quality but is highly convenient because it is in the public domain and is available online.

Hauptmann was cantor of St. Thomas's Church in Leipzig and thus was the direct musical descendant of Bach. He was a great friend of Felix Mendelssohn, who was instrumental in reviving interest in Bach with a performance of the *St. Matthew Passion* in St. Thomas's Church in 1839, and it is pleasant to speculate on what their conversations about Bach might have been like, perhaps conducted in the dusty archives of St. Thomas's itself.

Of course, the BWV (sometimes known as the *Neue Bach-Ausgabe* or NBA) edition is where one must turn for definitive versions of Bach's works. Many public libraries, and one would surmise most college and university libraries, have the BWV. The scores themselves are not downloadable, though the catalog is. Unfortunately, many of the NBA are out of print, and those that are in print are horribly expensive. It is no longer possible to buy a complete set.

Plenty of copies of the Mass in B Minor, the passions, and the *Christmas Oratorio* can be found in secondhand bookstores, and almost everything can be bought in individual scores, through various mail-order sheet music services.

BWV 1, *Wie schön leuchtet der Morgenstern* (How Brightly Shines the Morning Star)

This cantata was written in March 1725 for the feast of the Annunciation. With it, the second annual cantata cycle breaks off, incomplete. Christoph Wolff suggests that the anonymous librettist was Bach's neighbor and friend Andreas Stübel, who died in early March of that year (2000, 278). The piece ends an enormously productive period for Bach, in which he produced over forty cantatas in ten months, including some of his very finest, such as BWV 20, *O Ewigkeit, du Donnerwort*, with which the cycle opens; BWV 62, *Nun komm, der Heiden Heiland* [II] (Come Now, Savior of the Gentiles), which some think the greatest cantata of all; and BWV 180, *Schmücke dich, o liebe Seele*.

The founders of the Bach Gesellschaft (the forerunner of the BWV) chose this cantata for the first item in their catalog. They had intended to begin the catalog with the Mass in B Minor but were unable to acquire the manuscript. Instead they chose to start with ten of the most brilliant of the cantatas, and *Wie schön leuchtet der Morgenstern* was for them *primus inter pares.* They were perhaps influenced by the need to depict Bach as a colorful composer, the opposite of his reputation in the middle of the nineteenth century as a dry-as-dust writer of obscure fugues.

The chorale, very well known in Bach's time and still so, is by Phillip Nicolai. The plain setting of the chorale comes at the end of the cantata, as was often the case. It would be well to begin, however, by listening to this (BWV 1.6) setting, familiar and indeed singable by Bach's congregation.

Chorale, "Wie bin ich doch so herzlich froh" (I Am So Glad)
(CD Track 1)

Wie bin ich doch so herzlich froh,	I am so glad
Dass mein Schatz ist das A und O,	That my treasure is the A and O,
Der Anfang und das Ende;	The beginning and the ending;
Er wird mich doch zu seinem Preis	To his great praise
Aufnehmen in das Paradeis,	He will receive me into his paradise,
Des klopf ich in die Hände.	Which is why I now clap my hands.
Amen!	Amen!
Amen!	Amen!
Komm, du schöne Freudenkrone,	Come, you crown of joy, do not
bleib nicht lange,	delay,
Deiner wart ich mit Verlangen.	I wait for you with longing.

Some scholars hold that it is unlikely the congregation would have taken part. I prefer to imagine Bach swinging around in the Thomaskirche and imperiously bringing in the congregation with a deft flourish and a broad smile. Judge of their surprise when they heard one of the hunting horns that had spoken forth in the first movement (CD Track 2) now accompanying the melody line of this chorale, while the second horn rattled out a jaunty independent contrapuntal melody and the two oboes da caccia doubled the chorale's alto and tenor lines. It would be worth learning to sing the chorale melody, then the contrapuntal horn line. Before long, you would get a sense of how the two fit together. The last line of the chorale (1:04–1:13) consists of a simple descending scale of F major in the soprano line.

With the chorale in mind, turn now to the opening movement of BWV 1. We are in a festive but highly dignified world. The tempo is 12/8—four beats to the measure, with each beat further subdivided into three, the pace a slow but not solemn walk. Immediately, the orchestration strikes one as quite unusual, and it would have astonished Bach's audience. Besides the standard basso continuo and string parts (violas and cellos), we have three pairs of obbligato wind instruments; two violini piccoli sit at the top of the texture, sometimes doubling the ripieno violins but more often following their own solo lines. The violino piccolo was somewhat smaller than the standard violin and tuned four or even five half-notes higher. The violino piccolo is related to the *geige* or *kit*, favored by traveling musicians, which gave the dance form *gigue* its name. Bach wrote a violino piccolo part in the first "Brandenburg" concerto. Because the bow is short, the phrasing of the violino piccolo is always quite detached and decidedly jaunty. Below these in the concertino come two hunting horns pitched high (in F). These ancestors of the French horn were valveless. They are very difficult to play, but in Bach they always impart a sort of charming and spirited ungainliness. Below these (though higher in their natural range) are two oboes da caccia. The oboe da caccia is a spectacular beast, pitched a fifth below the oboe and curved through a full ninety degrees, rather like a giant sonorous cucumber. It was invented in about 1722, and Bach's is the first recorded use of the instrument. Some speculate that he had a hand in the conception of this curious instrument. The inversion of horns and oboes makes for an interesting sound; the horns strain like overambitious tenors, while the oboes quack like ducks. None of this is accidental; Bach wanted his first movement to sound rather like a country wedding, like something out of a Brueghel painting. Astonishingly for such a rich texture, every note can be heard clearly. Perhaps the unusual choice of tessitura helps in this.

A lengthy sinfonia or orchestral introduction precedes the vocal entries. It is worth listening to this first three minutes of music repeatedly. The continuo begins as it continues, with a dignified plod, and we hear the first violino piccolo (0:04), then the horns (0:09), then the second violino piccolo (0:13), then the horns again (0:17) for a more lengthy statement, then the oboes (0:32), then more horns, and finally all in tutti, before the sopranos open the chorale as a drawn-out cantus firmus (0:55). They are accompanied by alto, tenor, and bass in independent polyphonic phrases. Just before the second entry of the sopranos, however, tenors and then altos take a turn at the chorale melody, at twice the speed of the sopranos. One wonderful moment to listen for comes at 2:27, when we have what is termed a *suspension*, where the altos, sitting suspended on the note A, seem to get in the way of the sopranos, who come down from above to land on the B-flat one semitone higher and push the altos out of the way. The moment gives one quite a frisson. Listen always for these suspensions and passing dissonances, for Bach loved them and his music is full of them.

The whole movement is about nine minutes long and ends with a glittering harmonization of the final descending line of the chorale. It is followed in turn by a tenor recitative, then by a soprano and oboe da caccia duet, accompanied only by the continuo. After another recit comes a florid and joyful tenor aria, in which the violini piccoli duel with the orchestral violins in solo–tutti opposition, or ripieno–concertino, as Bach would have termed it. *Ripieno* means "full" or "stuffed," as in stuffed mushrooms.

BWV 5, *Wo soll ich fliehen hin?* (Where Shall I Flee?)

BWV 5 is full of surprises. It was written to illustrate aspects of the story of Christ curing a man who has palsy. The cantata is full of suffering and blood and pain. The first chorus, figuring the chorale as a cantus firmus in the soprano, with agitated string writing in sixteenth-notes, puts one in mind of moments in the *St. John Passion*. Like the opening chorus of the *St. John*, it is in the key of G minor, which often signals torment in Bach.

The theme of blood—the blood of suffering and of redemption—is raised in the recitative that follows the chorus, then developed in the third movement, a long tenor aria with what may be a rare example of a viola obbligato. This is far indeed from the violini piccoli of BWV 1. An unusual intensity comes from its being in the same tessitura or pitch range as the tenor solo, and the two lines compete in florid intensity. The alto recitative that follows is remarkable in placing the chorale melody above the singer, played by an oboe. The sense of security generated in this short recit is, however, dispelled when in the next movement, a da capo aria for bass, the devil enters, playing the trumpet, throwing around vulgar flourishes in the key of B-flat—an ironic and literally brazen challenge to the G minor tonality of the opening chorus. (B-flat major is the relative major key of G minor.) Raucous low staccato notes alternate with ungainly and uncomfortably high-pitched triplet figures. The devil tries everything, including military tattoo figures and indignant howls and yelps, but the soul will have none of it. Boldly marching straight ahead, he sings: "Verstumme, Höllenheer, / Du machst mich nicht verzagt!" (Be silent, host of hell, you will not make me despair). There is definitely a sense of the Christian having to place one foot firmly ahead of the other and not deviate to left or to right, whatever blandishments might intervene. Readers of Bunyan's *The Pilgrim's Progress* will recognize this dilemma and remember that it is not only the devil who can play the trumpet. Here is how Bunyan describes the end of Mr. Valiant for Truth: "When the day that he must go hence was come, many accompanied him to the River-side, into which as he went he said, Death, where is thy Sting? And as he went down deeper he said, Grave, where is thy Victory? So he passed over, and all the Trumpets sounded for him on the other side." Those trumpets are the ones Bach uses at the end of the Mass in B Minor. This is a da capo aria. Dramatically, this means that the devil gets to start over, at the return of the A section.

This astonishing aria is followed in a recitative by the voice of a child, unadorned save for the continuo accompaniment, singing, "Ich bin ja nur das kleinste Teil der Welt" (I am the tiniest fragment of the world). Bach's art is always dramatic, and in the case of this cantata it is theatrical also.

BWV 9, *Es ist das Heil uns kommen her* (Our Salvation Has Come to Us)

The biblical texts on which BWV 9 is based are not intrinsically dramatic; they are concerned with the rule of law and the resolution of disputes. These concerns are reflected in rather somber recitatives for bass. Beyond that, however, the music is full of joy and also passion. BWV 9.1 supplies the joy. This is a chorale fantasia with the hymn tune sung as a cantus firmus by the sopranos while the other three voices weave lively counterpoint under them. The vocal material comes in hymn-tune line lengths, interspersed with lively instrumental writing for strings with flute and oboe d'amore obbligatos. The key is E major—with four sharps this would lie at the outer edge of what is possible in the tonal world Bach inhabited before the age of equal temperament. The effect is to add a tartness to the sound. There is a flavor of the fourth "Brandenburg" concerto in the chattering woodwinds. A remarkable moment to listen for comes in the middle of the movement, when the writing for the lower voices becomes more homphonic and crisply staccato: the text here is "Der hat g'nug, g'nug, g'nug für uns all' gethan" (From him flow all, all, all our blessings).

BWV 9.3 is a tenor aria in E minor, with a violin obbligato part that makes heavy demands of the player. As you listen, pause to recollect that Bach rarely gave tempo indications. More often than not, the proper tempo is fairly clear. It is not so clear here. The time signature is 12/8, and when Bach writes sixteenth-notes he always intends that the tempo should be lively. The 12/8 meter in fact suggests that the aria may have the feel of a gigue, Bach's favorite dance, and the length of the lines entails breathing problems for the tenor soloist unless the music moves along. And yet the material is also quite somber. There is quite some divergence of opinion among various conductors. Helmut Rilling, for example, favors a somewhat tipsy dancelike tempo, while Harnoncourt prefers the sober approach. Some clue to how it might best go may be found in the C-sharp minor gigue-fugue in Book 2 of *The Well-Tempered Clavier*, which ought to trundle jovially along but should on no account be harum-scarum.

With BWV 9.5 the woodwinds return to accompany a soprano and alto duet. Their music has a remarkable lightness but an equally remarkable intricacy. The whole movement is a four-part canon, or rather a double canon, in which flute and oboe d'amore alternately lead and follow at a distance of a fifth below or a fourth above, while the soprano and alto perform identical maneuvers, but with different material. Listen to the first two minutes or so of this movement. Initially it may seem bewildering. One way to learn how to follow music such as this would be to concentrate on one line at a time. But first, notice that though this is a four-voice canon, a fifth line, supplied by the basso continuo, takes no part in the canonic weavings but rather supplies the harmonic underpinning with detached notes, mostly two to a measure. Get the sense of the music by listening first for that a few times. Then perhaps latch on to the tonality of the flute, for that is usually at the high point of the texture. Follow the flute's line as closely as you can, but be aware that the oboe has the same material, stated either after the flute or before it. Follow the same practice with the oboe, then with the soprano, then the alto. Before long you should be hearing the weaving together of the separate lines. Some people find it useful, when listening to complex fugal music, to take as many magic markers as there are musical lines and try to draw the patterns they hear. Or you could download the score and pick out the lines using different-colored highlighters. With a "short" score this exercise is a little tricky, for the flute and oboe lines will be presented on the one set of five lines, but it is doable.

Remember only that this is not music to be taken in entirely at first encounter, any more than a complex poem or a Rembrandt self-portrait would be. Rather, one studies, reflects, comes back.

As you listen, this is some of what you will find. Initially, the flute leads and the oboe follows; then the oboe shows the way to the flute. They come to their cadence and leave the coast clear for the singers—for the moment. The soprano enters, to be followed by the alto two seconds later. Soon, however, come paired entries on flute and oboe. The four voices now weave their way toward a cadence in E major (the dominant of the home key). Straight away, however, the obbligato instruments resume with another pair of entries. But shortly, the voices elbow their way in with their own pair of entries. Instrumentalists drop out for a while. And so it goes on, while we pause to consider some subject matter we have overlooked: What is it Bach is honoring? Faith over good works, it turns out. Not for nothing is he known as Bach the learned musician!

After the complexity of this four-part canon, Bach was right to end with as simple a harmonization of the chorale as possible.

BWV 20, *O Ewigkeit, du Donnerwort* [II] (O Eternity, You Thunderword)

BWV 20 was written for the opening Sunday in Bach's second cycle of cantatas, the first Sunday after Trinity, in June 1724. It consists of eleven numbers and was intended to be performed in two parts, before and after the sermon. The Gospel reading for the day (and therefore, one supposes, the sermon) has for its theme the fate that awaits the sinner who ignores the words of the prophets. This is a grim lesson, and for all its splendor this cantata displays some toughness. The cantata is based on the popular chorale "O Ewigkeit, du Donnerwort" (O Eternity, You Thunderword), which we hear in the first chorus and twice besides, before the sermon and at the end of the whole work. For such an elaborate work it is interesting that Bach provided very quiet and unadorned settings for the chorale. The chorale also furnishes the texts for the recitatives and arias. This cantata is not easy listening, if one pays attention to the text.

The opening chorus is most striking. Bach casts the first verse of the chorale in the form of a French overture. The French overture form (think of Jean-Baptiste Lully and Louis XIV) was traditionally the music accompanying the entrance of the French king into the opera. However, the earthly pomp is replaced by a sterner form of power: "O Schwert, das durch die Seele bohrt"—eternity is "the sword that bores into the soul." The French overture form has three sections: a grand, even pompous stately opening with dotted rhythms; a faster, fugal section; and at the end a return to the style of the opening material. In the case of the opening movement of BWV 20, the rhythm of the chorale changes. It is stated (as a cantus firmus, by the sopranos) first in common (4/4) time, then in triple time, and then again in 4/4. The harmonic writing is quite rich, and the orchestral texture is thickened by three oboes rather than the usual two. Remarkably, too, the haughty complacency of the double-dotted rhythm is disturbed by an intermittent quaking figure of repeated sixteenth-notes.

The whole cantata would certainly repay careful listening. Details to look for include a strange figure in the basso continuo under the word "ewig" (eternally) in 20.2 (tenor recitative). The orchestration of BWV 20.5 (a bass aria on the grim subject of God's eternal justice) is striking—three oboes and continuo, which most conductors assign to the bassoon. Are they being cheerful, and if so, why? Or is this a raucous cackling that Hieronymus Bosch would have understood?

The eighth number in the cantata is a bass aria with trumpet obbligato, and now the purpose of Bach's invocation of the French overture and all it stands for becomes plain. The trumpet is that of the Day of Judgment: "Wacht auf, wacht auf" (Wake up, wake up). One pities any poor parishioners who might have dozed off during the sermon. This aria would certainly rouse them, and they would likely stay awake for the alto recitative that follows and reminds listeners that even this very night the coffin cold be brought to their door.

BWV 21, *Ich hatte viel Bekümmernis* (I Had Much Heartache)

BWV 21 had its origin in Bach's Weimar years. We know it was performed in 1714 with the movements in the order we now have them. However, we do not know what these movements sounded like. The version we now have must have resulted from repeated revision, judging from the sophistication of some of the solo material, but the choruses especially contain material from very early in Bach's career. It was given in Leipzig in its present form in 1723, when Bach performed it in his first cantata cycle. In this final form it was the longest (almost forty minutes) of his cantatas and arguably one of his more complex. The Gospel reading that it illustrates is the parable of the lost sheep (Luke 15), and the epistle for the same Sunday recommends casting one's cares upon

God. However, Bach designated the work "per ogni tempo"—in other words, for any point in the church's year.

There is so much worthy of study in this cantata. It opens with a gracious sinfonia with some lovely duet material between violin and oboe. The first fugue pays tribute to a Vivaldi violin concerto and takes what seems to be a Vivaldi-like headlong course until interrupted in a dramatic way. BWV 21.9, the chorus "Sei nun wieder zufrieden" (Be at Peace, My Soul), is a chorale prelude with three vocal lines weaving in triple meter, up or down, or both together, around a cantus firmus chorale first in the tenor and then in the soprano line; BWV 21.8, with which the second part of the cantata begins, is a duet between Christ and the soul, for soprano and bass (the soul is always, in Bach, a soprano, and Christ is always a bass). This particular dialogue is enacted a number of times in Bach, most notably in BWV 140, *Wachet auf* (Sleepers, Wake), movements 3 (soprano–bass duet with violin obbligato) and 6 (with oboe obbligato).

But let us make a detailed study of just one movement from this grand work.

Chorus, "Das Lamm, das erwürget ist" (Worthy Is the Lamb That Was Slain) (CD Track 3)

The final chorus takes as its text the words from the Book of Revelation with which Bach's contemporary Handel chose to end his *Messiah*:

Das Lamm, das erwürget ist, ist würdig zu nehmen Kraft und Reichtum und Weisheit und Stärke und Ehre und Preis und Lob. Lob und Ehre und Preis und Gewalt sei unserm Gott von Ewigkeit zu Ewigkeit. Amen, Alleluja! (Rev. 5:12–13)	Worthy is the lamb that was slain, to receive power, and riches, and wisdom and strength, and honor and glory and praise. Praise and honor and glory and power be to our God forever and ever. Amen, Alleluia!

Bach's key is C major (the whole cantata has been in the general area of C and its related keys); Handel's key was the even brighter D major. But can there be much doubt that Handel knew Bach's earlier work?

There is considerable divergence among conductors about the tempo of this movement, and the disposition of forces. It would be worth sampling some of these differences. Bach Collegium Japan (BCJ), for instance, favors a very crisp tempo and has the whole work sung tutti. At such a tempo the sprightly sixteenth-note runs call for great control and precision, a call that BCJ nobly answers. Other performers choose a steadier tempo, and some assign portions of the vocal line to soloists. Harnoncourt is one such. Certainly, at the tempo Harnoncourt selects one can hear every detail. And given that eternity is the matter in question, one does not have a train to catch.

We begin with orchestral fanfares, supporting chordal blasts from the chorus. In just thirty-four seconds, Bach travels a considerable distance in changes of harmony.

What follows is a systematic analysis of the harmonic shifts in these thirty-four seconds. It would be worth listening several times to this passage, as it will help reinforce some important ideas about transposition and harmonic structure.

From C major (0:03) we travel via E major (0:08) to the relative minor key of A minor (0:13), pausing briefly there before embarking via D major (0:18) to the dominant major key of G (0:21), to move again three seconds later to B major (0:24) en route to E minor (0:28), which is the relative minor of the dominant key of G—a little more distant from the home key of C major, therefore. From E minor we go via G major (0:32) back to C (0:35), but not for long, for D major reappears (0:38) to take us again to G major, where we land on a welcome fermata (pause).

All that would furnish material for about two weeks study in composition 101; students studying modulation (traveling from key to key) are often directed to Bach for instruction. It is easier to hear than to understand on a strictly theoretical basis. But comprehension might flow were you to try to follow the chord progressions at a keyboard. If you do this, listen especially for what happens in the bass. If you do, you will find that the landing places are in what is called root position (where the name-note of the chord is at the bottom), sung by the basses and played by the continuo. Transitional chords, by contrast, are in what is termed the first inversion, which means that the "third" of the chord is at the bottom. For example, at 0:08 the E major chord sits on the note G-sharp in the bass.

At 0:43 the flavor switches from homophonic to polyphonic or contrapuntal, more specifically fugal. Now has come the time when we should somewhat systematically figure out what "fugue" is, for there is no shortage of fugues in Bach, whether in the forty-eight preludes and fugues (two in each of the major keys) known as *The Well-Tempered Clavier*, or in *Die Kunst der Fuge* (*The Art of the Fugue*), which Bach wrote at the end of his life, in response to a saucy upstart who had the nerve to suggest that the old boy was past it.

A fugue is a polyphonic composition, for two or more voices (sung or instrumental), in which one voice announces a subject (a short theme), which is answered by all other voices in succession. Most Bach choral fugues are for four voices, understandably. Some keyboard fugues are for two voices (for example, the two-part inventions), the majority for three or four voices, and a few (including some of the grander fugues in *The Well-Tempered Clavier*) for five voices. The whole matter of fugues is in fact astonishingly complex, but that is enough to start with, except to add in the concept of the countersubject, which is what the leading voice sings while the answering voice states the subject.

To make the concept of the countersubject clear, listen now to the fugue starting at 0:43 of BWV 21.11. The bass announces the subject at 0:43 and is answered by the tenor at 0:53. As you listen, try to hold on to what the bass is doing while the tenor starts in. You will hear a florid figure, in faster notes than the subject (sixteenth-notes as opposed to eighth-notes). This is the countersubject, and it provides some of the most interesting and important music in the whole fugue, as we shall see. In the case of this countersubject, we have three elements; the first two treat the word "Amen"—a sixteenth-figure that turns and tumbles downward but that ends with a shake figure, two notes repeated over and over, like a slow and mechanical trill. The third element, an arpeggio figure, rising then falling, colors the word "Alleluia." Every voice has the subject, in turn, and every voice follows its statement of the subject with this compound countersubject. Toward the end of the fugue, bewilderingly brilliant use is made of the three countersubject figures just described.

In the course of a fugue there will likely be several sets of entries. In the first and also the second set of entries in this fugue, the voices enter in order from bottom to top. This way of introducing the voices is not a requirement of the fugue, but it does make things slightly easier to follow. So we hear first bass (0:43), then tenor (0:57), then alto (1:02), then soprano (1:10). The cycle starts over at 1:19 with four more entries, in the same order, at approximately ten-second intervals The entries are equidistant. This is not always the case in Bach. Frequently, he will delay the third entry by some episodic material, which certainly arouses expectations. Often this episodic material arises from the countersubject.

This first set of entries has been accompanied by the basso continuo alone. Conventionally, this first set of entries is often taken by the solo voices, though there is no reason why it could not be sung by a semichorus (reduced numbers) or by the whole choir. However, there is no mistaking Bach's desire for a large statement at 0:20, for the trumpets and drums arrive, and now the call is certainly for the full chorus. Basses enter again, but now the sopranos are already busy with the countersubject, for in the first series theirs was the last entry and they have not yet had their say. The second set of entries follows in order, basses (1:19), tenors (1:29), altos (1:38), and sopranos (1:47).

At 1:54 the movement turns homeward; the interest now is with the countersubject material, and one voice after another scurries downward and around, every one at each other's heels and certainly hard to follow. There is some further reference to the subject in some chordal passages and one final bass entry (2:44), but the fun does not get going again, and the movement settles down to a series of emphatic C major flourishes.

That, then, is in rudimentary terms how a fugue works. It should be possible to take this sense of fugal structure and apply it elsewhere.

BWV 23, *Du wahrer Gott und Davids Sohn* (You True God and Son of David)

BWV 23 is often associated with BWV 22, *Jesu nahm zu sich die Zwölfe* (Jesus Gathered the Twelve Around Him); when he applied for the position of cantor at St. Thomas's Church in Leipzig, these were Bach's audition pieces. They contrast quite sharply with each other, and BWV 23 wins in the comparison as much the more far-reaching in its music and emotional range. The text itself has an outer and an inner theme. The outer one concerns the subject of salvation for all. The first movement, a double duet with two oboes and two singers, speaks of the universal provision of forgiveness. Then follows an act of individual mercy, the healing of the blind man described in St. John's Gospel, chapter 11. To depict this, Bach did something not unique but certainly remarkable; he wrote a recitative accompanied by strings and oboes, which place the Agnus Dei chorale "Christ du Lamm Gottes" at the top of the texture. This prepares the way for the final two movements. BWV 23.3 is a choral rondo, in which a tenor–bass duet alternates with choral passages. The theme unites universal salvation with the individual sufferings that have been healed in the recitative:

Aller Augen warten, Herr,	All eyes wait, almighty God, on
Du allmächtger Gott, auf dich,	you—and especially my own.
Und die meinen sonderlich.	

BWV 23.4, the last movement, is a large-scale chorale setting of the same hymn. It is a chorale prelude, or fantasia, in two sections, a grave beginning that would not be out of place in the *St. John Passion*, and a brisker section that marches steadfastly along. It is essentially a French overture.

BWV 34, *O ewiges Feuer, o Ursprung der Liebe* (O Eternal Fire, O Source of Love)

For performance at Pentecost, or Whitsunday, celebrating the descent to earth of the Holy Spirit, BWV 34 actually began life as a wedding cantata, and the air of good cheer and joy is appropriate to both. It is fairly simple in structure, with a massive trumpet chorus, a recitative and an alto aria with flute obbligato, another recit, and a final chorus.

The whole is definitely worth listening to carefully. For now, though, let us pick out one remarkable detail from the first movement. This is a trumpet chorus in D major. It is in triple time, three quarter-notes to a measure, more often than not subdivided into eighth-notes; thus the pulse is really 2 + 2 + 2. The chorus is a da capo movement, and the A section proceeds brightly but fairly uncontroversially in this three-in-one fashion. It is important to remember that Bach is writing for Pentecost and therefore celebrating the establishment of the Trinity.

Then comes the surprise. Before Bach's time, and since, musicians have been fascinated with the commutative principle, which provides among other things that three times two is the same as two times three. To see what this might mean, one can recall Leonard Bernstein's lyrics to the song "America" from *West Side Story*: "I want to be in America." First, "I want to be in A-" falls naturally into two groups of three quarter-notes, with the stresses on "I" and "be." Then "me-ri-ca" falls into three pairs of two quarter-notes. Sing the line over repeatedly and beat on the table and you will immediately grasp this idea, perhaps counting 1 2 3 1 2 3 1 2 1 2 1 2. It is as if (for those who remember about rhythm) one had alternating measures of 6/8 and 3/4. The technical term for this transition of three groups of two into two groups of three is *hemiola*, and Bach employed it all the time. In the *Goldberg Variations*, for example, thirty variations on a simple melody in triple time, Bach is constantly resubdividing as outlined above, and there is even one movement written out in triple time that makes sense only if you play it the other way (6/8 instead of 3/4), for the first few measures—that is, until Bach switches the stressing on you.

To hear the hemiola at work, listen to BWV 34.1. This is one of Bach's largest trumpet choruses and at first sounds like straight-ahead music. It is a da capo piece. Listen for a moment toward the end of the A section. You will find the spot. Try tapping a foot or drumming a finger, in three or two as necessary. Notice that sometimes you will need to be drumming in two and three at the same time, as vocalists and instrumentalists quarrel with each other about whether they are in two time or three. Of course, the trumpets win in the end as the A section returns and triple-time order is restored.

BWV 36, *Schwingt freudich euch empor* (Soar Joyfully Upward)

BWV 36 developed by fits and starts. It started out as a secular cantata and went through a number of iterations before Bach converted it into a sacred cantata for use on the first Sunday in Advent. It is full of incident. From an instrumental point of view, the first movement feels like an oboe concerto in the Telemann mode; the vocal lines are in clear contrast, with irrepressibly jaunty, leaping lines, blocked outburst to the words "Doch haltet ein!" (But stop for a moment!). The duet for soprano and alto that follows is based on the great chorale "Num komm, der Heiden Heiland." The texture is very open, the accompaniment for basso continuo and oboes (doubling the vocal lines) alone. Part 1 of the cantata ends with a lovely setting of "Wie schön leuchtet der Morgenstern," the chorale on which BWV 1 was based. This version has some graceful but not obtrusive decorations to the melody. It is in the slightly more forgiving key of D (BWV 1 was in F major), which would suggest that it would be sung by all, just before the sermon. The oboes figure prominently in a tenor aria in Part 2, chattering away in sixteenth-notes while the tenor soloist sings a chorale verse as a cantus firmus. But the high point of this cantata must surely be the soprano aria (BWV 36.5) with muted violin obbligato, audaciously taking its cue from the text:

Auch mit gedämpften, schwachen Stimmen Wird Gottes Majestät verehrt.	Also with muted, weak voices Will God's majesty be honored.

There are frequently surprises in Bach.

BWV 39, *Brich dem Hungrigen dein Brot* (Break Your Bread for the Hungry)

Breaking bread for the hungry is the charge laid on the listener in this huge cantata, which is definitely among Bach's finest. The opening chorus is in several sections, of which the first is especially moving. It is in triple time, with steady quarter-notes, rather plodding beats in the

basso continuo, while two flutes and two oboes and the violins alternate
with pairs of staccato eighths. They are clearly full of meaning. What
are they? The tears of the hungry? Faint cries? They seem to surround
us with imperatives. The sounds are certainly something eternal, and
this is music to live with and to live by. The texture livens and broadens
at the words "Führe ins haus" (Bring him into your house). It is as if
one opened one's arms. A fugue begins with the words "So du einen
nackend siehst" (If you see a naked person, clothe him). The final fugal
section of the movement presents in long melismata the rewards that
come to the righteous: "Alsdenn wird dein Licht herfür brechen wie die
Morgenröte" (Then will your light break forth like the dawn).

After the obligatory didactic bass recitative, three strongly con-
trasted arias and an alto recitative follow. There is an alto aria with two
obbligato lines, from violin and oboe. The voice and obbligato instruments are in much the same tessitura (range), and the effect is quite
warm in feel. The bass aria that follows is stark, accompanied only by
basso continuo, its message simple: "Wohlzutun und mitzuteilen verges-
set nicht; denn solche Opfer gefallen Gott wohl" (Do not forget to do
good and to share, because such an offering pleases God). Having fed
and clothed the hungry, and served one's own soul by doing so, what is
God's portion? As often in Bach, this Lutheran severity is tempered by
a soprano aria, often the childlike voice of the soul, and an alto recitative seems to speak of the here and now.

BWV 41, *Jesu, nun sei gepreiset* (Jesus Now Be Praised)

BWV 41, a cantata for the new year, is full of cheerfulness but certainly
has some surprises. It opens with a long chorale chorus featuring three
trumpets, drums, and three oboes, along with the usual strings and
basso continuo. The opening chorus lasts about eight minutes, and
within that space there is considerable variety. It is one of the finest
trumpet choruses but is a trumpet chorus nevertheless.

What follows is astonishing. First, there is a soprano aria with all three oboes cackling along. It is in 6/8 time, and though not quite up to dance tempo, it really is a jig—Bach's favorite dance, as his audience must have well known; was the Kappellmeister as he conducted about to cut a caper down the aisle?

One wonders whether the purpose of this charming but fairly light number may have been to set the stage for what follows. BWV 41.4 is a tenor aria with violoncello piccolo obbligato. The cello piccolo was a favorite instrument of Bach's. It was one of a range of lower stringed instruments that did not make it into the modern world, though one can still find them. This distinguished group of losers included the viola da braccia, as well as the arpeggione (a six-stringed behemoth for which Schubert wrote one of his greatest works), and one might even count the viola da gamba, though one still meets that individual socially from time to time. The piccolo cello had either five strings—the standard four tuned on C, G, D, and A, with a fifth string tuned to the high E—or four, in which case the lowest (C) string was omitted. In this aria, the lowest string is not needed. The unincluded C string is by no means a constraint; the obbligato line is all huge leaps and bold swirls. It is a da capo aria, and in the B section the obbligato has patches of silence, then dramatic intrusions—as is sometimes the case in a da capo aria. There is more about the piccolo cello later, in the treatment of BWV 180.

Perhaps most surprising of all for us, and certainly for Bach's audience, is BWV 41.5, which sets out as a plausibly straightforward Bach recitative, with a startling intrusion from the chorus, who hammer out a response from Luther's litany, of a not particularly nice kind:

Doch weil der Feind bei Tag und Nacht	Yet since by day and night
Zu unserm Schaden wacht	the enemy looks to harm us,
Und unsre Ruhe will verstören,	and to disturb our rest,
So wollest du, o Herre Gott, erhören,	may You, Lord God, listen
Wenn wir in heiliger Gemeine beten:	when we pray:
Den Satan unter unsre Füße treten.	"Crush Satan under our feet."

Also worth looking at—for it, too, makes use of Luther's litany—is Cantata 18. It contains several passages of cursing that call for alternative language in these pluralist times, if otherwise politically naive baroque musicians should wish to avoid getting into a Salman Rushdie–type situation. It is not often performed.

BWV 41 ends with a restatement of its chorale, with trumpet commentary. It goes into triple time partway through but ends with a foursquare recollection of the opening number.

Thirty Selected Cantatas, Second Group

In this next group of ten cantatas, we have one of the most massive and spectacular cantatas, BWV 42; two solo cantatas, BWV 51 and BWV 56; and the arrival of some visitors riding camels, in BWV 65.

BWV 42, *Am Abend der desselbigen Sabbats* (On the Evening, However, of That Same Sabbath . . .)

This long and unusually splendid cantata was written for the first Sunday after Easter, in 1725. The author of the libretto is unknown. It deals with the appearance of the risen Christ to his disciples. Particularly wonderful is the opening Sinfonia, lasting between five and a half and six minutes, depending on the pace. There are several recordings: John Eliot Gardner's is very sprightly; Harnoncourt's is a little puddingy for my taste. Once again, I favor Masaaki Suzuki with Bach Collegium Japan for the whole cantata, but especially this opening sinfonia, scored for two oboes, bassoon, strings, and continuo. The oboes and bassoon form a concertino, obbligato group—there is a separate continuo line of which the bassoon is not a part. It feels rather like a movement from a lost concerto, with distinct divisions into concertino and ripieno. Bach's challenge was to provide a cantata for a "low" Sunday—the first after Easter, with the potential for anticlimax, and this sinfonia is a fine start. It should be noted that the other Quasimodogeniti cantata (as the first Sunday after Easter used to be called), BWV 67, *Halt im Gedächtnis Jesum Christ* (Keep Jesus Christ in Mind), is another cantata of high quality. The late Craig Smith felt that either of these two cantatas is finer than anything Bach wrote for the feast of Easter itself. BWV 67 is discussed in the following paragraphs. The drama of the cantata is quite acute. Musically, the question is, What can happen after Easter? The disciples have a parallel question: What now? What is it to be alone?

The oboes and bassoon figure also in BWV 42.3, a long alto aria in da capo form. The concertino instruments are silent in the B section, which has the additional unusual characteristic of switching from the adagio common measure into a more pastoral and relaxed 12/8. This is followed by a curious duet (marked "chorale," since it takes its text from one) for tenor and soprano, with a burbling bassoon obbligato. The texture of the vocal lines is quite spiky. Then comes a duet marked "chorale" for tenor and soprano accompanied by bassoon, cello, and continuo. A relatively short but enormously busy bass aria follows, calling for virtuosic singing. The chorus has not figured so far, but in 42.7 they sing a large Lutheran chorale, which ends with a most beautiful Amen:

Verleih uns Frieden gnädiglich,	Graciously grant us peace,
Herr Gott, zu unsern Zeiten;	Lord God, in our time;
Es ist doch ja kein andrer nicht,	there is indeed no other
Der für uns könnte streiten,	who could fight for us
Denn du, unser Gott, alleine.	than You, our God, alone.
Gib unsern Fürsten und all'r Obrigkeit	Give our rulers and all lawgivers
Fried und gut Regiment,	peace and good government,
Daß wir unter ihnen	that under them
Ein geruhig und stilles Leben führen mögen	we might lead a quiet and peaceful life
In aller Gottseligkeit und Ehrbarkeit.	in all blessedness and honor.
Amen.	Amen.

BWV 51, *Jauchzet Gott in allen Landen* (Praise God in Every Land)

This solo cantata was written rather late, in 1730. It is one of a large number of solo cantatas written about this time, and a number of commentators, of whom Schweitzer was an early one, have suggested

that this can be explained by recalling that the choir at St. Thomas's
Church was in some disrepair around that time. The cantata is apparently attached to Trinity 15 but is marked "per ogni tempo." Some
think that the music is beyond the intellectual and musical range of a
boy soprano. I concur with a number of writers in believing that it must
have been written for performance by a woman, and various plausible
candidates have been proposed, among them of course Bach's own wife
Anna Magdalena Bach. The trumpet writing in the first and last is so
florid and confident that only a soprano capable of equaling a baroque
trumpet could survive. Many thrilling recorded performances of this
cantata are available—as well as some pretty shoddy ones. Again,
Bach Collegium Japan with Carolyn Sampson are terrific; unusually,
she has to contend not only with a trumpet, but also with what sounds
like a trombone or hunting horn in the continuo line. Harnoncourt's
recording is wonderful, as is Rilling's. Lucia Popp makes it sound like
Puccini, and in Schwarzkopf I do believe one can discern, beyond the
trumpet, the clank of spear against Viking helmet. This cantata seems
to be something everyone feels they have to have a go at. Top of the list
for me, however, is a performance by the Aston Magna Foundation,
with Sharon Baker as soprano soloist.

There are five movements, of which the first and last have the trumpet obbligato. The cantata is in C major and related keys. BWV 51.1 is
a da capo aria with an elaborate trumpet obbligato, containing difficult
high runs and rapid repeated notes. The soprano line calls for great agility and range; it takes the soloist up to high C, two octaves above middle
C. There is a gentle aria in 12/8 (a siciliano, which we will learn about
when we consider movement 1 of BWV 244, the *St. Matthew Passion*.
A chorale in the fourth movement has a pair of lively obbligato violins.
The final movement sets just one word, *Alleluia*, and can be heard as CD
Track 4. There are quite a number of solo cantatas, including several for
alto voice (BWV 54, *Widerstehe doch der Sünde*; BWV 170, *Vergnügte
Ruh, beliebte Seelenlust*), for bass (BWV 56, *Ich will den Kreuzstab
gerne tragen*; BWV 82, *Ich habe genug*—I Have Enough), and for tenor
(BWV 55, *Ich armer Mensch*—I, Wretched Man). The solo cantatas
are not frequently performed, perhaps because they spread performing
opportunities rather sparsely around; choirs (who put on concerts) like

to sing. The rarity of their performance is a pity, because the music is usually spectacular, as may be heard in the last movement of BWV 51, which will have to represent all of Bach's solo cantatas.

Aria (soprano), "Alleluia," with trumpet obbligato (CD Track 4)

This short movement opens with the soprano; there is no instrumental ritornello, and indeed, the trumpet obbligato does not start until after the first vocal statement (0:05). The soprano and trumpet duet together for a little while, until both leave the action and a we hear a busy string interlude, which the trumpet joins (0:44) after almost thirty seconds of silence—quite a long absence in such a short movement. The trumpet resumes, followed shortly by the soprano, and in a change of character the word *alleluia* is sung twice, on a detached arpeggio, at 1:01–1:04 and 1:05–1:08, the latter taking the singer up to high C again (though just the once in this movement). Further florid meanderings from the soprano support the trumpeter, who has his own arpeggio passages, and we are out after only a little more than two minutes, trumpeter and soprano for a well-deserved drink, one hopes.

BWV 56, *Ich will den Kreuzstab gerne tragen* (I Will Gladly Carry the Cross)

If BWV 51 is a necessary item in the soprano repertoire, the same can certainly be said for the baritone repertoire and BWV 56, known as the "Kreuzstab" cantata—with this difference, that BWV 51, fabulous enough to be sure, has an undeniable air of fluff about it. On a 1988 album called *A Bride's Guide to Wedding Music*, BWV 51 is lined up among the usual suspects: Pachelbel's Canon in D, Liszt's *Liebestraum*, Rachmaninoff's *Vocalise*, and Elgar's *Salut d'amour*. The Kreuzstab cantata is on an altogether higher level, however.

All the great baritones have recorded the Kreuzstab cantata, most of them several times. Dietrich Fischer-Dieskau recorded it for the first time in 1951 on Archiv and several times since, signally with Rilling in 1983. Gérard Souzay and Hermann Prey each recorded it in 1959, Souzay recording it for a second time in 1968, Prey returning to it in 1987. John Shirley-Quirk, the English baritone, recorded it in 1965 with the Academy of St. Martin's in the Fields under Neville Marriner. Despite my great admiration for Fischer-Dieskau, Shirley-Quirk's is my favorite performance. The Decca recording is still available, and the Kreuzstab cantata is paired with another great baritone cantata, BWV 82, *Ich habe genug*. The two cantatas are often paired together. Other great performances include Max van Egmond with Brüggen in 1977, Thomas Quasthoff in 2004, and Peter Kooy with the Bach Collegium Japan in 2008.

One of the challenges for the singer in this cantata is the length of the phrases. The first movement, in steady triple time in G minor, opens with a lengthy ritornello featuring an obbligato oboe. (Oboes often play long phrases, owing to the ability of oboists to breathe in and out at the same time. It almost seems, sometimes, as though they can inhale through orifices unknown to the rest of us.) The first vocal phrase calls for eight measures without a break, starting with the difficult series of rising notes D, G, B-flat, C-sharp, and D, then going on to several series of paired eighth-note "sospiri." At the end of these eleven measures there is perhaps room for a quick breath before setting off on a further ten measures, leading to the relative major B-flat cadence. The whole first section of the aria must be sung on what is essentially one good breath and a couple of furtive gasps. The sospiri represent, of course, the grunts and tears of the suffering individual who carries the cross of suffering. The cantata was written for Trinity 19, when the Gospel is taken from the ninth chapter of *Matthew*, when Jesus heals the sick. Though not generally discussed, it does seem to me that Bach also had in mind the carrying of the cross by Simon of Cyrene, as depicted so movingly and memorably in the *St. Matthew Passion*. Again, there is more than one suggestion that Bach was punning on the word *Kreuzstab*, which also was the name of a precursor of the sextant, picking up on Jesus's boat journey on the Sea of Galilee. BWV 56.2 is a recitative that depicts the waves that may have rocked the boat. The cello continuo plays sixteenth-note arpeggios throughout. Movement 3 is a brisk aria in B-flat major with a sprightly oboe obbligato, somewhat reminiscent of the final soprano–bass duet in BWV 140, *Wachet auf.* There is one more recitative, with arioso, which ends with a long melismatic setting of the word *Tränen* (tears) before a final chorale for SATB.

This is certainly a cantata one should seize the chance of hearing, along with *Ich habe genug* and BWV 55, *Ich armer Mensch*, other great solo cantatas for male voice.

BWV 60, *O Ewigkeit, du Donnerwort* [I] (O Eternity, You Thunderword)

This cantata, written for the twenty-fourth Sunday after Trinity in 1723, is cast in the form of a dialogue between Fear and Hope. Probably because it fit with the existential angst of the age, this cantata was enormously popular in Vienna at the turn of the nineteenth century. Kokoschka, an angst-ridden fellow if ever there was one, made a series of lithographs in 1914 based on the cantata, of which Plate 4, *A woman guiding a man*, and plate 7, *Fear and Hope; a man comforting a woman*, are particularly well known. Most people see a resemblance between the woman in these plates and Alma Mahler, the wife of the great composer Gustav Mahler; she had a passionate relationship with Oscar Kokoschka. Then in 1935 Alban Berg quoted the final chorale in the last movement of his violin concerto *In Memory of an Angel*. The Berg concerto is based on a twelve-tone row, the last four notes of which are the first four notes of the chorale with which Bach's cantata ends. The last four notes of the row, ascending whole tones, are also the first four notes of the final chorale melody, "Es ist genug" (It Is Enough). The angel in question brings Alma Mahler back into the picture, for she was Manon Gropius, Alma's daughter, and the first performance was intended to be a memorial to her. How the gods thwart us! Poor Berg died, of an unromantic bee sting, before he could hear the first performance, and so the violin concerto turned out to be the last thing he wrote and was performed as his own memorial.

In this cantata, Fear is played by the alto soloist and Hope by the tenor, though the Holy Ghost also makes an appearance at the end, sung by a bass soloist. There are a small number of other duet or dialogue cantatas, including BWV 57 and BWV 58, both of which are most interesting. BWV 66, described below, though not completely in the form of a dialogue cantata, does also contain dialogues between Fear and Hope. But BWV 60 is by far the best known.

In the first movement, the alto soloist is confined to a chorale, while the tenor weaves elaborately around this. They are accompanied by two oboes d'amore in concertino, and a hunting horn doubling the chorale, as well as the standard strings and continuo, and an orchestra consisting of natural horn, a pair of oboe d'amore, strings, and basso continuo. The concertino group is joined by a piccolo violin in the third number, and the alto soloist is visited by the voice of the Holy Ghost in the fourth movement, as a bass soloist who in three closely similar arioso passages, first in D, then in E, then finally in C, sings of the blessedness of the dead, extending the thought progressively in the second and third entries, specifying that the happy dead are those who die in the Lord. Fair enough, one might observe. It certainly silences the soprano, whose grieving has gone on for quite some time. And that is the thought Bach closes with, by using the chorale "Es ist genug" (It Is Enough), certainly echoing the last word of Christ on the cross and ending this nervy dialogue.

BWV 63, *Christen, ätzet diesen Tag* (Christians, Etch This Day in Metal and Marble)

We turn now to a much less agonized work, a Christmas Day cantata likely from Bach's Leipzig period (1714), performed also in Leipzig in 1723 and perhaps again in 1729. The work is ambitious in every way. Bach had just been promoted to the position of Weimar's concertmaster, from that of organist, and this new post gave rise to a number of cantatas, this one included—the first Christmas cantata Bach wrote, and equal to anything else Bach did for Christmas, cantatas making up the *Christmas Oratorio* included. The scoring is for four soloists, four-part chorus, four trumpets, timpani, three oboes, bassoon, first and second violins, viola, organ, and continuo. Two of the arias are duets—the first for soprano and bass, the second for alto and tenor. The first chorus, in triple time, in C major, is as classy a trumpet chorus as one could wish for. The high point, however, is the long accompanied recitative for alto that follows this first chorus; another accompanied recitative for bass, coming just before the final chorale chorus, is also impressive. The final chorus has the bravura of the first, but with an additional element of thoughtfulness, variety, and depth. The cantata is an interesting mixture of the gleeful and the reflective.

BWV 65, *Sie werden aus Saba alle kommen* (They Will All Come Forth Out of Sheba)

When he was appointed to the position at Leipzig, Bach was specifically asked not to write theatrical music. One wonders what the authorities thought of the opening number of this cantata, written in 1724 for the Feast of the Epiphany. It concerns the visit of the Wise Men (or Magi) to the stable where Jesus was born. The opening chorus is in a loping 9/8 that sounds plodding even if one attends to the underlying three in a bar; and pairs of horns in C (unique in Bach), recorders, and oboes da caccia lend a decidedly exotic flavor to the music, leading many of us to think of camels. The visitors, though, seem not to be just the Magi, but all of us, as the text of the opening movement definitely seems to indicate. The first four vocal entries are in a sense fugal, but they are identical in pitches, not in the familiar tonic–dominant alternation, and there is a striking unison passage right at the end, unison for both voices and instruments.

Unusually, there follows a lovely Christmas chorale in triple time. It is unusual for a chorale to be placed so early, and it seems to me to reinforce the communal nature of the visit to the manger. Then follows a long recitative for bass that meditates on the gifts brought by the Magi but goes on to ask, What do the poor bring? The answer: Only their hearts. The singer's is definitely a human voice. The poor person's heart is also the theme of the wonderful song by Peter Cornelius about the three kings in which a baritone aria is accompanied by "Wie schön leuchtet der Morgenstern," the chorale on which BWV 1 is based. This recitative is followed by an aria, also for bass, which has a wonderful canon for the two oboes. There is then a recitative/aria pair for tenor, the aria of which is a jolly dance, a minuet, it seems to me. Of course, there is a concluding chorale, one of the better-known ones, even to us today. The congregation must have left St. Thomas's skipping.

BWV 66, *Erfreut euch, ihr Herzen* (Rejoice, You Hearts)

This cantata was likely first performed on Easter Monday 1724 in Leipzig. It started out, however, in Weimar, as a birthday cantata for Prince Leopold. This now lost work is cataloged as BWV 66A. BWV 66 is thus a parody. *Parody* is the term used to describe quoting oneself by recycling material. Bach's music is full of such parodies, and when one hears some unusually splendid orchestral music in the cantatas (as for example in the glorious sinfonia in BWV 42, already mentioned), one can suspect self-borrowing, sometimes justifiably so. Sometimes Bach is parodying lost material, as here. Sometimes one can find the source. BWV 52, *Falsche Welt, dir trau ich nicht!*, has a long sinfonia that we know better as the first movement of the first "Brandenburg" concerto; several movements of the B Minor Mass initially were heard in other works, as for example the Gratias agimus section of the Gloria, which first saw light as the opening chorus of BWV 29, *Wir danken dir* (We Thank You, O God). The opening chorus of the present cantata is an unusually grand da capo piece, over eight minutes long, with trumpet and two oboes in elaborate sixteenth-note flourishes and tricky violin passages in thirty-seconds.

As noted earlier, in the discussion of BWV 60 (*O Ewigkeit*), BWV 66 can be classed among the dialogue cantatas. We hear some dialogue between alto and tenor in the middle section of this opening chorus and a dramatic dialogue between Fear and Hope in the fourth section, a recitative for alto and tenor, which is continued in a 12/8 duet with violin obbligato and continuo. This movement is really a gigue (see the discussion of Joseph of Arimathea's aria, no. 65, in the chapter on the *St. Matthew Passion*).

BWV 67, Halt im Gedächtnis Jesum Christ (Keep Jesus Christ in Mind)

This is one of the shorter cantatas, about twelve minutes long, but made up of seven numbers. It is one of two written for Quasimodogeniti, or the first Sunday after Easter. The other, BWV 42, has already been discussed. This cantata deals with the story of Doubting Thomas. The earlier of the two was first performed in April 1724 and so falls in the first annual cycle of cantatas. Two other wonderful cantatas come from the same post-Easter period that year, BWV 104, *Du Hirte Israel, höre,* and BWV 166, *Wo gehest du hin?* (Where Do You Go?). The opening chorus is a brief but brilliant invocation of Easter, of the resurrection, featuring what Bach describes as a "corno di tirassi," likely a slide trumpet. This is followed by a lively, dancelike tenor aria, with obbligato oboe d'amore. In the middle we have a chorale framed by two alto recitatives. The most startling piece of the cantata, and one of the real landmarks of the whole Bach choral repertoire, is the sixth number, in which a bass soloist sings the blessing of peace of the risen Christ. As he does so, the chorus proclaims the defeat of Satan, but there is a good deal of tension, not least in Jesus's last proclamation of peace, dissipated in the end by a marvelously serene orchestral passage.

BWV 75, Die Elenden sollen essen (The Wretched Shall Eat)

This long and spectacular work was the first piece performed by Bach after his arrival to take the post of cantor in Leipzig in 1723. He evidently meant to make rather a splash; this cantata encompasses fourteen movements and was intended to be performed in two parts, before and after the sermon. The next Sunday he gave another massive work, BWV 76, also in fourteen parts, to be discussed next.

The opening chorus is cast in the form of a French overture. The opening slow section is in triple time, with dotted rhythms throughout and an expansive oboe obbligato. It occupies three of the total five minutes of the chorus, giving way to a brisker fugal section in common time. So much about this cantata is wonderful, and perhaps the most surprising is the sinfonia that opens the second half, in which Bach takes the chorale heard at the end of the first part and gives it to the solo trumpet over an elaborate string ritornello. We hear the chorale again, "Was Gott tut, das ist wohlgetan" (What God Does Is Well Done), at the end of the whole work. Especially wonderful also is the bass aria with trumpet obbligato and ripieno strings, toward the end of the cantata—"Mein Herze glaubt und liebt" (My Heart Believes and Adores).

BWV 76, *Die Himmel erzählen die Ehre Gottes* (The Heavens Declare the Glory of God)

The congregation in Leipzig, awestruck, one trusts, by the preceding cantata, came back for more of the same the next week and heard BWV 76. This cantata, also in two parts, lasts over one hour. It begins with a trumpet chorus—of course. But there is a difference. This movement is scored for intermingled solo and chorus singing, and babbling along with the trumpet is an obbligato oboe d'amore, which is somehow expected to hold its own. The tempo of the movement is and should be quite steady, what Bach and Handel would have called "tempo ordinario." The first half contains two fine arias, the second of which is a bass aria with trumpet obbligato, calling for some florid work from the singer as well as from the trumpet.

The second half of the cantata opens with a movement that displays great novelty in the scoring; it features two obbligato instruments, the oboe d'amore and the viola da gamba, a combination not heard before in Bach's cantatas. The treatment is novel, though the music occurs elsewhere—in one of the organ trio sonatas (BWV 528). The gamba was to go on to figure prominently in the two passions, especially the *St. Matthew Passion.*

Thirty Selected Cantatas, Third Group

BWV 83, *Erfreute Zeit im neuen Bunde* (Joyful Time in the New Covenant)

Written for the festival of the Purification of the Virgin Mary and perfomed for the first time in Leipzig in 1724, this cantata begins by focusing on Mary rather than on the subject of the Nunc dimittis, the aged Simeon, who is the subject of the second number. BWV 158, *Der Friede sei mit dir* (Peace Be with You), discussed below, is wholly Simeon's, especially the aria "Welt, ade" (World, Farewell).

BWV 83, written in F major and in 4/4 time, is essentially a solo cantata, with an opening aria for alto, with an elaborate orchestral accompaniment for six obbligato instruments (two horns, two oboes, solo violin), and with full ripieno strings and continuo. It is hard work for the alto just to hold up against such massive forces. Bach Collegium Japan's version is wonderful. Neither Rilling's (Helen Watts) nor Harnoncourt's (unnamed boy alto) version makes it against any of those featuring countertenor Robin Blaze or Bach Collegium Japan countertenor Robin Tyson, nor against Eliot Gardiner's versions or the Ton Koopman–conducted one with Austrian mezzo-soprano Elisabeth von Magnus (Amsterdam Baroque Orchestra and Choir). In orchestral texture this movement reminds one of the first movement of "Brandenburg" concerto no. 1.

BWV 83.2, termed "Intonazione e recitativo," is for bass and takes its text from the Nunc dimittis, the aged Simeon's farewell to the world after he has seen the young Jesus. It is scored for strings. It calls for accomplished legato singing from the bass soloist.

BWV 83.3 is a gigue with a virtuosic violin obbligato and an athletic tenor line. This da capo aria in F major is marked in common time (4/4) but, like other similar pieces, is really in 8/8, with each beat divided into three, so it really can be thought of as being in compound measure with a time signature of 24/16. It is a full six minutes of dance, on the subject of hastening to one's salvation, thematically complementing and amplifying Simeon's farewell.

BWV 96, *Herr Christ, der einge Gottessohn* (Lord Christ, Only Son of God)

Written for Trinity 18 and performed in October of 1724, this is one of the most cheerful of Bach's cantatas, permeated with dance rhythms. The opening chorus is a sort of skittish pastorale, echoing BWV 1 and the *Christmas Oratorio*'s pastoral music. Even in those portions of the text that dwell on death, the happy prospect of the hereafter is brought to the fore. The orchestration is for transverse flute, piccolo flute (or sopranino recorder), piccolo violin, two oboes, and two violins. There are no violas, and Bach calls for horn and trombone in the continuo. This is quite an unusual configuration, and we must remember that nothing in Bach's music is accidental.

The first chorus is a brisk 9/8, in F major, with a skittering sopranino recorder obbligato (termed by Bach *piccolo flute*), and a cantus firmus chorale in the alto. This movement has some of the flavor of BWV 1, a resemblance confirmed halfway through the present chorus, when the text refers to the morning star. The chorale is doubled in the alto by a high trombone called *tromba da tirassi*, and this versatility in orchestration also reminds one of BWV 1, where Bach went to great pains to have instruments playing on the edge of their normal range, for solid thematic purposes. The transverse flute supplies the obbligato in the third movement, a da capo tenor aria with the feel of a gavotte, with, however, some tension, found in the complex harmonic shifts of the middle section. The bass aria is more somber and purposeful, yet even in this D minor aria in triple time there is something of the dance. The tempo is that of the minuet; the bass soloist is asking God to be accompanied to heaven's door, and the sense of God's courtly attentiveness is depicted in the rhythm. Note especially the staccato passage (marked thus by Bach) in the middle section.

BWV 97, *In allen meinen Taten* (In All My Actions)

This is one of the longer cantatas, at about thirty minutes. The late Craig Smith, in a commentary for Emmanuel Music, suggested that Bach cast the cantata in the form of a baroque suite. By this hypothesis, we have a French overture, followed by a gigue, then an allemande such as one might find in an English suite—one of the gravest dance forms. Movement 8 is a gavotte. BWV 97 is quite late in date (1734), though it clearly incorporates material from much earlier. No occasion is specified, though Schweitzer suggests, without much authority, that it may have been a wedding cantata. The text is taken from the hymn "Innsbruck, ich muss dich lassen" (Innsbruck, I Must Leave You).

The opening movement, in B-flat, does have all the identifying signs of a French overture, with a stately slow section characterized by dotted-note groupings, followed by a stately but driving fugal section, with the chorale as a cantus firmus in the alto. This movement puts me in mind of the opening movement of the C minor keyboard partita.

In contrast, and in the relative minor key of G minor, is the gigue-like second movement, which is sparsely treated, for bass soloist and basso continuo. The continuo line in the middle section is remarkably lyrical, however.

BWV 97.4 is an astonishing movement, a long tenor aria with a violin obbligato of taxing dimensions, featuring complex melismatic passages and double stopping. It feels like earlier material, from Cöthen or Weimar perhaps, certainly from a time when Bach had access to the kind of talent likely to be able to do justice to this piece.

Also of note are a soprano–bass duet with continuo and an aria for alto with two oboes, gavotte-like, as has already been suggested.

The cantata ends with a simple treatment of the wonderful chorale.

BWV 100, *Was Gott tut, das ist wohlgetan* (What God Does Is Well Done)

Also dating from the 1730s (and perhaps the latest surviving cantata) is this cantata possibly intended for Trinity 15.2. It calls for some virtuosity, both from the vocal soloists (who are employed in a duet and three arias) and from the orchestra, featuring horns, timpani, transverse flute, oboes d'amore, strings, and continuo. The subject is God's comfort and the joy that derives from it.

The opening chorus is taken from an earlier cantata (BWV 99, of 1724). It has some very detailed and tricky orchestral writing, for obbligato flute and two oboes, and some discreet observations from the timpani. There is a cantus firmus chorale in the soprano line, reinforced by a brass instrument (cornetto), as was Bach's common practice. There are long instrumental interludes between the chorus entries.

Other wonderful instrumental treatments are found in the soprano aria (BWV 100.3) with a flute obbligato, and an alto aria (movement 5) with an introductory oboe d'amore solo. Vocal feats of a high order are called for in the bass aria (movement 4), which has wide leaps and complex syncopated rhythms. The final chorale, with trumpet and drum fanfares, is adapted from cantata BWV 75, *Die Elenden sollen essen*, considered earlier.

BWV 104, *Du Hirte Israel, höre* (You Shepherd of Israel, Hear)

The best word to describe this cantata is *gorgeous*. It was written in 1724, for the second Sunday after Easter. The Gospel for that day is from John 10 and tells the parable of the Good Shepherd—the day is still known as Good Shepherd Sunday. The music is pastoral and very approachable. It played an important role in the revival of interest in Bach's work in the early years of the nineteenth century. A volume of six cantatas (which came to be designated BWV 101–6) was published in Germany and led to the Bach revival whose centerpiece was the performance of the *St. Matthew Passion* in 1829 by the twenty-year-old

Mendelssohn. He loved this cantata, and we can hear that admiration in the opening number, which was the model for the chorus "He Watching Over Israel" from *Elijah*. We can, I believe, also hear the influence of this number in Mendelssohn's duet "Ich wollte mein Lieb" (I Would That My Love Could Silently Flow in a Single Word, op. 63.1). Mendelssohn's song is full of passages of thirds and sixths moving in parallel. Then again, when two voices move strictly in parallel, thirds and sixths are about all you have. That said, Bach does it beautifully in this chorus, as you will shortly hear.

Chorus, "Du Hirte Israel, höre" (You Shepherd of Israel, Hear)
(CD Track 5)

This is pastoral music, and Bach goes to great lengths to give it that bucolic air. The continuo opens with seven three-beat measures of low G, like a bagpipe drone. Above this, the two oboes and their big brother the taille, or tenor oboe, have staccato chords, marked with dots by Bach. Against this, the strings have a continuous rippling figure in triplets and dotted pairs, so the movement, a pastorale, though marked 3/4, is really in compound, 9/8 time. These staccato notes in the oboes anticipate the chorus's treatment of the words *höre* (listen) and *erscheine* (appear). When the chorus enters, the continuo line sits on the drone note for twelve measures, and later on for seven, then five, then another five measures. Bach marks the violin writing carefully with phrasing. This is emphatically not a gigue, and so the groups of triplets are marked to be phrased as threes, not in the two-plus-one style of the giga (this idea is discussed in detail in the commentary on no. 65 of the *St. Matthew Passion*, in Chapter 7).

The chorus is followed by two paired recitative–aria groups, for tenor, then for bass. BWV 104.3, for tenor, oboe d'amore obbligato, and basso continuo, is especially impressive in its word painting—with a particularly long melisma on the word *lange*. BWV 104.5 is a pastorale aria for bass in 12/8, with the oboe d'amore doubling the violins, pitched quite low, and quacking, rather. The cantata ends with the chorale "Der Herr ist mein getreue Hirt" (The Lord Is My True Shepherd).

BWV 105, *Herr, gehe nicht ins Gericht mit deinem Knecht* (Lord, Do Not Pass Judgment on Your Servant)

First performed in 1723 (Trinity 9), this work is based on a psalm verse and has for its theme the burden of sin. The first chorus and the fifth movement are both very substantial ones, and the third is rather unusual.

BWV 105.1 is a two-part chorus in G minor, the first a slow section in triple time in which the continuo line plays repeated eighth-notes throughout, moving, if at all, on each pulse. Over this we hear several groups of entries from the chorus, at one quarter-note's distance from each other, on the word *Herr* (Lord). "Herr, gehe nicht ins Gericht mit deinem Knecht. Denn vor dir wird kein Lebendiger gerecht" (Lord, enter not into judgment with thy servant, for in your sight shall no man living be justified). The first, slow section deals with the first half of the verse, and there follows a brisk fugue (marked in two-pulse, the so-called cut time) with the second half of the verse as text. Movement 3 is a soprano aria with obbligato oboe and strings. Like BWV 244.49, the "Aus liebe" aria from the *St. Matthew Passion*, but like very little else in Bach, there is no continuo line; the scoring is for oboe obbligato, violins 1 and 2, and viola. The soprano line contains several runs scored in thirty-second-notes. The aria's subject is the difficulties presented to the conscience in a world of waverers, and this wavering is depicted with vivid musical imagery. The fifth movement of the cantata is a stalwart, marchlike da capo aria for tenor, inquiring, "Kann ich nur Jesum mir zum Freunde machen?" The sentiment here is: If only Jesus can be my friend, Mammon and the world's other inducements will present no problems. The aria has a virtuoso violin obbligato, as well as what Bach describes as a *Coronet* or *Kornett* (probably terms for the corno da caccia, which Bach often used to reinforce melody lines in need of emphasis, as in BWV 140.1, discussed in the following section); these pick up the vocal melody here and there. There is an adaptation of this aria for soprano, sung by Kathleen Battle, with the violin obbligato played by Itzhak Perlman. It is pitched up a minor third, but even so it is a performance to marvel at and is available on Deutsche Grammophon.

BWV 140, *Wachet auf, ruft uns die Stimme* (Awake, Calls the Voice to Us)

Wachet auf (Sleepers, Wake) is one of the best-known Bach cantatas, and if one had to choose a sole representative for the genre, this would probably be it. The subject is the parable of the wise and foolish virgins; the wise virgins are those who keep their lamps trimmed in preparation for the arrival of the bridegroom. It feels like an advent cantata, and in a sense it almost is. It was written for the twenty-seventh Sunday after Trinity, a day that occurs only rarely in the church calendar and that in most years would in fact be Advent 1. It was written for that day in 1731 and thus appears very late in Bach's cantata production. It is a large-scale work. The cantata, in E-flat and related keys, begins with a long chorus with the chorale "Wachet auf" as a cantus firmus in the soprano (doubled by horn or corno da caccia—the watchman's trumpet), rather in the manner of the opening chorus of the *St. Matthew Passion*. The key choice is important; it takes the chorale melody up to high G at its big moment. This first chorus is in triple time, with counterpoised concertino groups of strings and woodwind (two oboes and a taille, or tenor oboe). There is a fugal middle section on the word *Alleluia* for the three lower voices, with the cantus firmus returning with the same word. The voice of the night watchman is heard in a recitativo secco, then follows the first of two soprano and bass duets, dialogues between the soul and Christ. In C minor, it has a virtuoso violino piccolo obbligato; the soprano calls out, over and over, "When will you come?" and the bass responds with the reassurance sought: "Ich komme." The violino piccolo was tuned a minor third higher than the standard violin tuning, and Bach treated it here as a transposing instrument, writing the part out in C (= E-flat). The second, in B-flat major, has a gavotte-like flavor, with a lovely oboe obbligato. *My friend is mine*, sings the soprano; *I am indeed yours*, sings the bass. Between the two is perhaps the best-known movement, a chorale fantasia for tutti tenors (the text speaks of the watchmen [plural] singing), obbligato unison strings (violins and viola), and continuo. It is the only movement from which Bach excluded the violino piccolo. That he added violas to the violins tells us he had a particularly rich effect in mind. The piece was published in 1747 as the first of the "Schübler" organ chorales (BWV 645). The cantata ends with a plain setting of the cantata, in one of Bach's grandest harmonizations and orchestrations.

BWV 147, *Herz und Mund und Tat und Leben* (Heart and Mouth and Deed and Life)

This cantata was first performed in Leipzig in 1723, on the Feast of the Visitation of the Blessed Virgin Mary. Much of the music dates from the Weimar period, as part of one of a series of Advent cantatas. It could not be performed during Advent in Leipzig because of the penitential nature of the season, so it was reassigned. At the same time, Bach added recitatives (all accompanied, and unusually fine) and also the famous chorale fantasia that ends both Part 1 and Part 2.

When I was searching for the perfect ensemble to do the CD for this book, with my mind on Nicholas Harnoncourt, I watched online streaming videos to marvel at the master conducting the first, and some other, movements from BWV 147. Then by chance, following a link, I found a video of Bach Collegium Japan performing this cantata, and the question was immediately settled. We have two tracks from this wonderful cantata on our CD, the first chorus, because it is so classy, and the last movement, which is a chorale fantasia known to many, perhaps to all, as "Jesu, Joy of Man's Desiring," because, well, just because you can't not. There are some pieces of music that act as a mirror for humanity, and this is one of them. At Christmastime, even if you can somehow dodge "The Little Drummer Boy," you certainly won't escape for long without hearing some version or another of this Bach chorale fantasy. Weddings aren't safe, either, nor first-grade recorder recitals. It may be the most recorded tune ever. Olivia Newton-John, Josh Groban, Kiri Te Kanawa, the Church Organ All Stars, the Modern Mandolin Quartet, James Galway (of course), Leo Kottke, the Bluegrass Worship Band, Elmo, the Red Army Choir and Orchestra, Bill and Gloria Gaither and their Homecoming Friends, Pete Seeger, the Bands of the Salvation Army, the Trinidad and Tobago Steel Band, the Yuletide Hicks, the Celtic Christmas Singers, the Cape Cod Wind Ensemble, and a karaoke version by Stingray Music; all these artists have put their mark on this veritable fire hydrant of a chorale fantasia. I did not find a reggae or a klezmer version, but that does not mean they don't exist. I rather thought the Klezmonauts might have put it on their Christmas compilation *Oy to the World*, but they didn't.

The piece itself is quite wonderful and surprising in a number of ways. For example, who would have thought that soulful melody, in its tender, lilting 9/8, was a rather raucous oboe obbligato, and that the soprano line of the chorale is doubled by the trumpet? The 9/8 tempo has to move along; this movement is not exactly a gigue, but nor is it a siciliano. A pastorale, maybe. It has to go fast enough for the choir to be able to sing long, full lines without running short of breath. Remember that it is not the only chorale fantasia in the cantatas; the one that ends BWV 22, also with an oboe obbligato, is every bit as good.

Chorus, "Herz und Mund und Tat und Leben" (Heart and Mouth and Deed and Life) (CD Track 6)

Herz und Mund und Tat und Leben	Heart and mouth and deed and life
Muss von Christo Zeugnis geben	Must for Christ bear witness
Ohne Furcht und Heuchelei,	Without fear and falsity
Dass er Gott und Heiland sei.	That he God and Savior is.

The opening chorus is in C major, with strings, continuo, two oboes, and a trumpet obbligato, played on a tromba da tirassi or slide trumpet. The tempo is a steady allegro, in four. A hearty ritornello opens the piece, figuring the trumpet prominently. The melody announced by the trumpet has eighth-notes that are essentially skipwise figures arpeggiated upward and downward, and stepwise sixteenth-note runs that twist backward and forward (0:03–0:10). The air of cheerfulness is palpable, mirroring the uncomplicated conviction of the text. There is new material in a threefold sequence at 0:11 through 0:22 and a slight development or variant on it at 0:24 and 0:26, with contrapuntal echoes in the continuo line, before the top line skitters down the scale from high C to treble C for the cadence and the entry of the sopranos at 0:34. The entries are fugal, sopranos starting on C, answered at a distance of one measure by the altos, beginning on the fifth. The tenor entry, back to C, is delayed by one measure to make room for a brief episode (such a delay between the second and third voices is very common in Bach). The basses get in one measure later, and we are, as they say, off. The sopranos make what appears to be the start of a further fugal set at 1:02, but this turns out to be what is termed a false entry, leading to episodic material; there is a lovely moment just there, lovely because simple, when the altos sing a downward descending scale, to be answered a measure later (1:04) by the basses, who lead to a perfect cadence in the home key of C major. Then at 1:08 and again at 1:12 we see the fruits of the arpeggio material from the opening sinfonia, and also the three-fold sequence for orchestra described earlier, when the sopranos sing a phrase that must count as one of the most cheerful pieces of melody in all music. All voices take this up, and soon the sopranos and altos in thirds, echoed at the distance of a quarter-note by the lower two lines, announce a stepwise figure, which they have alone a few moments later as they drift up to high G before at 1:29 a sort of shadow comes across the texture with a brief reference to fear and doubt, and we move into the territory of A minor, the relative minor of the home key. At 1:43 a brief orchestral interlude presents the opening material, but now with a minor tonality. Things pick up again at 1:50 with the arpeggio material, basses and tenors now, to be answered by the upper voices after half a measure at 1:53. The music turns very chromatic, and the sensation of trepidation returns at 2:11 to continue through several measures of development before a cadence in the subdominant, which always brings a slackening of tension.

We now have a second full set of fugal entries, much as before, two pairs of entries (bass and tenor first this time), a measure's delay, then the second pair, alto and soprano. This last entry, at 3:00, ends with a busy passage of three measures, consisting largely of sixteenth-notes, in the soprano, before the last entry of the arpeggio figure at 3:15 leads us, through some very full vocal writing, to the final ritornello at 3:41. This last soprano entry is absolutely magical.

There are four arias, for soprano, alto, tenor, and bass, each seem-ingly better than the last. My favorite is the long soprano da capo aria, no. 5, in D minor, in compound time—marked C, but it is really 8/8, with each beat subdivided into three sixteenth-notes. It is really a gigue.

Gigue-like also is the famous chorale fantasia, though perhaps the tempo should be a little slacker than the term suggests. It certainly cannot be allowed to be slushy.

Chorale fantasia, "Jesus bleibet meine Freude" (Jesus Will Remain My Gladness) (CD Track 7)

Jesus bleibet meine Freude,	Jesus will remain my gladness,
Meines Herzens Trost und Saft,	Essence of my heart, its hope;
Jesus wehret allem Leide,	Jesus from all grief protecteth,
Er ist meines Lebens Kraft,	He is of my life its strength,
Meiner Augen Lust und Sonne,	Of mine eyes the sun and pleasure,
Meiner Seele Schatz und Wonne;	Of my soul the joy and treasure;
Darum lass ich Jesum nicht	Therefore I will Jesus not
Aus dem Herzen und Gesicht.	From my heart and sight allow.

The continuo plods solidly along throughout, three notes to the measure; against this strings and oboes weave a nine-note-per-measure texture—this for a square eight measures, when the chorus enters (0:19) homophonically for the first four-measure line of the chorale. The soprano line is doubled by the trumpet. As they come to rest on the dominant chord of D, the orchestra enters again, essentially decorating the fermata at the end of the chorale's first line. The second line begins at 0:31, and when this ends, the orchestra repeats the first material (0:39) and brings back the chorus for the next two lines, musically identical to the first two. The ritornello resumes at 1:16, but its last measure takes us now solidly into the dominant key of D major. At 1:35 the chorus reenters with line 5 of the chorale, modulating to A minor in four measures, and the orchestra then picks up again in that key (1:42 to 1:50). From A minor to C major is a short step, and this is where the next four measures of the chorale go (line 6). The instruments bluff in the direction of the flat keys, seeming to be headed to F major via a passing B-flat, but then the oboe makes a counterbid with an F-sharp and we are back in the home key of G major for the last two lines of the

chorale at 2:04 and 2:24. At this point, the continuo settles on a tonic
pedal, under some passing harmonies rather reminiscent of the end of
the first prelude of Book 1 of *The Well-Tempered Clavier*, before at 2:34
reprising the last eight measures of the first ritornello, and we are out.

BWV 158, *Der Friede sei mit dir* (Peace Be with You)

This is an odd work. It is very short, consisting only of an aria and a
chorale, each with a preceding recitative. Perhaps there was a larger
work, or at any rate a larger conception. It is not know when it was
written or performed. A manuscript not in Bach's hand notes that it is
suitable for an Easter service or for the Feast of the Purification of the
Virgin Mary. The bass aria (with tutti soprano chorale and an astonishingly elaborate violin obbligato), "Welt ade" (World, Farewell), is
reason enough to attend to it carefully, though it is rarely performed.
The violin solo lies very high and was probably written for the violino
piccolo so beloved of Bach. This aria feels as though it might belong
in one of the passions. If intended for the Feast of the Purification, its
focus is much more on the aged Simeon than on the Virgin Mary. For
a contrast, see BWV 83, *Erfreute Zeit im neuen Bunde*, discussed at the
beginning of this chapter.

BWV 180, *Schmücke dich, o liebe Seele* (Adorn Yourself, O Dear Soul)

This brings us to the last of our thirty selected cantatas. The cantata
was written for Trinity 20 and draws its theme from the Gospel for that
day: Many are called, but few are chosen. It is on a large scale; BWV
180.1, the first chorus, is over seven minutes long, and the tenor aria
that follows is almost as long. The chorale itself, heard both in a plain
setting at the end and as a cantus firmus in the opening chorus, is one
of the most beautiful.

The orchestration is especially detailed: two recorders, two transverse flutes, oboe, oboe da caccia, violoncello piccolo, two violins,

viola, continuo. The orchestra is put to good use in the first chorus, a fairly quick pastorale, not a little gigue-like, in 12/8 time, with an ambling, almost staccato basso continuo line, four notes to the measure for the most part, with antiphonal choirs of oboes, flutes, and strings in a continuous sixteenth-note colloquy.

A recitative/arioso combination (movement 3) for alto features a piccolo cello. The arioso is a modestly decorated version of the chorale, in triple time, with an obbligato for the piccolo cello in flowing sixteenth-notes. It is not clear precisely what Bach means by "piccolo cello." Some contend that it is an instrument with the four lowest strings in the standard cello tuning with an extra string at the top, tuned also a fifth above its neighbor, therefore to E. It is possible that the sixth Bach cello suite was written for an instrument such as this. Others hold that it was a sort of viola on steroids, held on the right, not left, shoulder. Museums house a huge variety of odd instruments, some of which made it into the musical mainstream, others not. A Canadian cellist, Josephine van Lier of Edmonton, has inquired deeply into this whole question of the violoncello piccolo and plays an instrument that is roughly the size of a thee-quarter-size cello, with the extra fifth string. She writes, on her fascinating Web site, "Playing this little cello is a very special experience. Its sound is in many ways closer to that of a viola da gamba. The high e-string gives it a little bit of a 'silver' sound, rather than the 'golden' sound often used to describe the cello's sonority." I can recommend two lovely recordings of the number. Bach Collegium Japan's version is predictably wonderful. Yukari Nonoshita is the soprano, as so often in BCJ's Bach series. Also very good is that of La Petite Bande, with the fabulous Belgian soprano Sophie Karthauser. In either of these performances one can hear the cello piccolo clearly. Bach's writing for it in the obbligato is wide in range, and the soprano chorale sits comfortably in the middle range, and so the two sounds seem to overlap a little. This is one of the many fascinating scoring effects in this cantata.

The transverse flute obbligato in the tenor aria (movement 2) is also especially lovely, and the aria is taxing for the tenor soloist. A little shorter, though also remarkable, is BWV 180.5, a soprano aria in B-flat,

"Lebens Sonne" (Sun of Life), in triple time, with a striding continuo line, six to the measure, and an oboe obbligato.

The final chorale is beautifully understated. No elaborate orchestration is needed. Bach clearly loved this chorale. He wrote a great organ chorale prelude based on it, BWV 654, also in E-flat. This treatment originated in 1708–17, but Bach returned to the revision of the "Great Eighteen" chorales in 1739–42. E-flat is a key Bach was fond of. He returned to it often, especially in the two passions. It is the key of another great cantata, BWV 140, *Wachet auf*—and the associated chorale prelude BWV 645, the first of the "Schübler" chorales—and seems to be a key in which it would be appropriate to conclude our discussion of the great Bach cantatas.

St. John Passion

We have two complete extant passions by Bach, the *St. Matthew Passion* (BWV 244) and the *St. John Passion* (BWV 245). The word *passion* comes from the Latin word for suffering, and a passion tells the story of the suffering and death of Christ. There were some other passions; C. P. E. Bach, in his obituary of his father, states that there were five. There may have been an early passion written during the Weimar period. If so it is lost, but it is at least possible that some of that material resurfaced in the *St. John* and *St. Matthew*. The *St. John* was completed in a first version in 1724 but was revised several times thereafter. The *St. Matthew* dated from 1727–29. There is a *St. Luke Passion* dated about 1730, the manuscript of which is in part by Bach, though the music is certainly not. Finally, there was a *St. Mark Passion* (1731), now lost. Though lost, it does have its BWV number—BWV 247. So the situation is somewhat tantalizing; Bach may have offered Leipzig a much wider treatment of the Holy Week story than we can now envisage, or perhaps he had grander plans in mind than he was able to carry through. We simply do not know, but even so, the two extant passions offer more than enough to command our attention.

The *St. John Passion* was initially performed in Leipzig on his first Good Friday there, in 1724. A certain amount of uproar surrounded the first performance; unknown to the newcomer Bach, the tradition was for the Good Friday presentations to alternate between St. Thomas's Church and St. Nicholas's Church. Bach innocently scheduled the 1724 event for St. Thomas's, but at the last moment he was instructed to move the performance to St. Nicholas, after having already printed the librettos. There were space problems in the new venue, and Bach complained that the harpsichord in St. Nicholas's was in disrepair. The whole entertaining story is told by Wolff in *Johann Sebastian Bach: The Learned Musician* (2000). Apparently, the forces were cramped. A memorandum (NBR, 145ff) of 1730 gives insight into the scale of forces required for such a production—at least thirty-six performers, counting singers and instrumentalists.

Bach performed the *St. John* again in 1725, this time at St. Thomas's. It was much revised, and he revised again in about 1730. It later received yet one more revision, and this final fourth version, finished sometime in the 1740s, is the one we now usually hear, as represented by several items on our CD.

Without the background provided by the program of cantata writing on which he had embarked, the composition of the passions would not have been easy. In the passions we have all the elements worked out in the cantatas—recitative, aria, arioso, and chorus. The two-part *St. John Passion* feels like a pair of cantatas, writ large. The sections were separated by a sermon, as was also the case with many of the large-scale cantatas. For Bach's audience it would all have seemed very recognizable.

The text is based on the Gospel of John, chapters 18 and 19. With the biblical material there is a body of commentary, explanation, and meditation based on poetry by a number of librettists, chief among whom was one Barthold Heinrich Brockes, author in 1712 of a very popular pietistic poem, *Der für die Sünden der Welt gemarterte und sterbende Jesus* (Jesus Tortured and Dying for the Sins of the World). Woven among the whole are eleven chorales, all well known in Bach's time, some still known today, and all beautiful, none more so than the lovely "In meines Herzens Grunde," still sung today in Protestant churches to the words "All glory, laud, and honor, to thee redeemer King."

We will consider the *St. John Passion* in two sections, as it was intended to be heard (with an intervening sermon). I shall preface the commentary on each part with the biblical text.

Part 1 takes the action up to the highly dramatic denial of Peter, when the music breaks off for the sermon. (The following extracts are from the Revised Standard Version of the Bible.)

St. John Passion, Part I, text

When Jesus had spoken these words, he went forth with his disciples across the Kidron valley, where there was a garden, which he and his disciples entered.

Now Judas, who betrayed him, also knew the place; for Jesus often met there with his disciples.

So Judas, procuring a band of soldiers and some officers from the chief priests and the Pharisees, went there with lanterns and torches and weapons.

Then Jesus, knowing all that was to befall him, came forward and said to them, "Whom do you seek?"

They answered him, "Jesus of Nazareth." Jesus said to them, "I am he." Judas, who betrayed him, was standing with them.

When he said to them, "I am he," they drew back and fell to the ground.

Again he asked them, "Whom do you seek?" And they said, "Jesus of Nazareth."

Jesus answered, "I told you that I am he; so, if you seek me, let these men go."

This was to fulfill the word which he had spoken, "Of those whom thou gavest me I lost not one."

Then Simon Peter, having a sword, drew it and struck the high priest's slave and cut off his right ear. The slave's name was Malchus. Jesus said to Peter, "Put your sword into its sheath; shall I not drink the cup which the Father has given me?"

So the band of soldiers and their captain and the officers of the Jews seized Jesus and bound him.

First they led him to Annas; for he was the father-in-law of Caiaphas, who was high priest that year.

It was Caiaphas who had given counsel to the Jews that it was expedient that one man should die for the people.

Simon Peter followed Jesus, and so did another disciple. As this disciple was known to the high priest, he entered the court of the high priest along with Jesus, while Peter stood outside at the door.

So the other disciple, who was known to the high priest, went out and spoke to the maid who kept the door, and brought Peter in. The maid who kept the door said to Peter, "Are not you also one of this man's disciples?" He said, "I am not."

Now the servants and officers had made a charcoal fire, because it was cold, and they were standing and warming themselves; Peter also was with them, standing and warming himself.

The high priest then questioned Jesus about his disciples and his teaching.

Jesus answered him, "I have spoken openly to the world; I have always taught in synagogues and in the temple, where all Jews come together; I have said nothing secretly. Why do you ask me? Ask those who have heard me, what I said to them; they know what I said."

When he had said this, one of the officers standing by struck Jesus with his hand, saying, "Is that how you answer the high priest?"

Jesus answered him, "If I have spoken wrongly, bear witness to the wrong; but if I have spoken rightly, why do you strike me?"

Annas then sent him bound to Caiaphas the high priest.

Now Simon Peter was standing and warming himself. They said to him, "Are not you also one of his disciples?" He denied it and said, "I am not."

One of the servants of the high priest, a kinsman of the man whose ear Peter had cut off, asked, "Did I not see you in the garden with him?" Peter again denied it; and at once the cock crowed.

Part 1 opens with a long (approximately nine-minute) chorus, for full forces, likely including vocal soloists as well as the ripieno chorus. Bach himself noted in the memorandum, referred to earlier, that the practicalities of producing such a large-scale work with largely amateur forces made it necessary to split chorus work up into tutti (ripieno) and solo (concertino) groups. This chorus is in da capo (ABA) form, and the B section is often performed by the vocal soloists. The emotional temperature of this chorus is high, fueled by a sixteenth-note ostinato figure in the strings running through practically the whole movement. The key is G minor, always hot in psychological temperature in Bach. (At this point, it would be useful to compare this with the opening of the *St. Matthew Passion*, which is quite different in feel, altogether more coolly liturgical. It is CD Track 13.) The opening chorus of the

St. John Passion starts with an ostinato figure, two instrumental lines each consisting of flute doubled by oboe weaving long, slow, discordant figures. Note for example their first entries; the first line starts on the note D, and half a measure later the second line enters at the distance of one semitone, in what is known as an *unprepared suspension*. Bach's instrumental genius is seen in his choice of forces here; two of anything on one note is always apt to sound astringent—this is why in a string ensemble at least three players per line is recommended, and you need three singers per part minimum in a chorus. Bach clearly wanted the sourness we find here. The text begins by praising the Lord; the middle section foreshadows the suffering that waits. The text of this chorus was a piece of free verse (author unknown). The passion narrative is now taken up in the first recitative, which may be heard as CD Track 8.

Recitative (Evangelist, Jesus), "Jesus ging mit seinen Jüngern" (Jesus Went With His Disciples), with choral interjections
(CD Track 8)

Evangelist: Jesus ging mit seinen Jüngern über den Bach Kidron, da war ein Garten, darein ging Jesus und seine Jünger. Judas aber, der ihn verriet, wusste den Ort auch, denn Jesus versammlete sich oft daselbst mit seinen Jüngern. Da nun Judas zu sich hatte genommen die Schar und der Hohenpriester und Pharisäer Diener, kommt er dahin mit Fackeln, Lampen und mit Waffen. Als nun Jesus wusste alles, was ihm begegnen sollte, ging er hinaus und sprach zu ihnen:

Jesus: Wen suchet ihr?

Evangelist: Sie antworteten ihm:

Chorus: Jesum von Nazareth.

Evangelist: Jesus went with his disciples over the brook Kidron, where there was a garden, which Jesus entered with his disciples. But Judas, who had betrayed him, also knew the place, for Jesus had often assembled there with his disciples. When Judas had procured for himself the crowd and the chief priests and the Pharisees' servants, he entered there with torches, lanterns, and weapons. Now as Jesus knew all that he must encounter, he went outside and said to them:

Jesus: Whom do ye seek?

Evangelist: They answered him:

Chorus: Jesus of Nazareth.

Evangelist: Jesus spricht zu ihnen:

Jesus: Ich bin's.

Evangelist: Judas aber, der ihn verriet, stund auch bei ihnen. Als nun Jesus zu ihnen sprach: Ich bin's, wichen sie zurücke und fielen zu Boden. Da fragete er sie abermal:

Jesus: Wen suchet ihr?

Evangelist: Sie aber sprachen:

Chorus: Jesum von Nazareth.

Evangelist: Jesus antwortete:

Jesus: Ich hab's euch gesagt, dass ich's sei, suchet ihr denn mich, so lasset diese gehen!

Evangelist: Jesus said to them:

Jesus: I am he.

Evangelist: Judas also, who had betrayed him, stood beside them. And when Jesus had said to them, "I am he," they drew back and fell to the ground. Then he asked them for a second time:

Jesus: Whom do ye seek?

Evangelist: And they answered:

Chorus: Jesus of Nazareth.

Evangelist: Jesus answered:

Jesus: I have told you that I am he; if ye seek me, let these people go.

The narrative in both passions is in the hands of the Evangelist (tenor), with the roles of Jesus, Peter, and others taken by other soloists. Usually, the tenor Evangelist will not also be the singer of the tenor arias; the role is too demanding and calls for different vocal characteristics. The range of the Evangelist is both high and wide. In the present example, for instance, it goes from tenor E-flat (a sixth below middle C) to middle A (a sixth above middle C) and sits generally high, for the most part above middle C. The singer's goal will always be flexibility and a general impression of artlessness. Recitatives are almost always accompanied by continuo alone—in the case of our example, by cello and harpsichord, though any other continuo instruments, for example bassoon and organ, or even lute, would serve equally well. The current favoring of harpsichord and cello derives from the practice stipulated by C. P. E. Bach, but there is no need for performers to be bound to this preference.

We open over a sustained chord of C minor—one step toward the flat side of the key pattern from the G minor of the opening chorus, and the first phrases, describing the visit by Jesus and his disciples over the brook Kidron to a garden, stay with this tonality and close with a perfect cadence (the V chord to the I chord), often used as a decisive punctuation mark in a Bach recitative (0:01–0:16). In the first of many narrative surprises, the tonality shifts to a strange chord, known as a Neapolitan sixth and by various other names. This highly dramatic— even melodramatic—chord consists of two overlapping, discordant tritones; in Bach's time and after, the tritone was also known as "the devil's chord," so it is appropriate that it should color the entry into the action of Judas, the betrayer of Christ. The tenor sings in the middle to the lower end of the range, and his first three notes, D-flat, B-flat, G, constituting the tritone, are as blunt a statement of impending evil as Bach could muster (0:18–0:19). It seems Judas is not with the initial party, for we learn that he also knew the place, as a popular resort of Jesus and his friends, as the narrator goes on to say, in a phrase ending with another perfect cadence, this time in F minor, yet one step more toward the flat side (0:33). He has gathered together what amounts to a posse, sent to him by the chief priests and the Pharisees (whose complicity in the impending evil is painted with its own colorful tritone at 0:37–0:39). The group arrives with torches, lanterns, and weapons. The focus turns to Jesus, and the tonality follows, in the stable and not-in-the-least discordant key of B-flat, often associated in Bach's music with an air of pastoral grace (0:51–1:04). Then comes a dramatic surprise: we hear the V chord and expect the standard perfect cadence, the full stop. Instead, we hear what is known as an *interrupted cadence*, leading us not to the established tranquility of B-flat major, but back to the G minor of the opening chorus, the key of suffering (1:04–1:06), as we hear Jesus for the first time asking the mean whom they seek. The answer comes from the chorus, representing now not the faithful (as was the case in the opening chorus), but the aggressors. The orchestral texture once again consists of busy sixteenth-notes; the chorus texture is rather crudely homophonic, depicting the mentality of the herd, who are already at the point where a call for blood would not be surprising (1:09–1:18). Taking the initiative, Jesus identifies himself with what seems like a morally clear perfect cadence (1:24–1:25), but another reference to Judas, again painted with the colors of the devil's chord (1:30), undermines the equilibrium instead. Jesus's words have caused all present to shrink backward and fall to the ground, at which he repeats his initial question, with the same vocal notes but in a different tonality (1:52–1:54), leading this time to the key of C minor (one step away from G minor, toward the flat side) and the crowd's second outburst, similar to the first (1:56–2:04). A brief recitative, in which Jesus asks that since they have found their quarry they should let the disciples go, ends our extract and brings us back to the reassuring key of B-flat major, releasing all tension, seemingly (2:06–2:22).

The first of many chorales ensues ("O grosse Lieb"—O Wondrous Love), celebrating the love of God in giving himself up to suffering while we cherish earthly pleasures. The chorale is in G minor; the reference to living in "Lust und Freuden" is colored in the key of B-flat, and the effect is quite surprising, as is the dramatic recoil back to G minor at the end of the chorale. Did Bach expect or hope that the congregation would join in this chorale? Probably not, for the melody of this quite well-known chorale is elaborately modified. But it would certainly sound like familiar ground after all the drama of the preceding music, and it prepares well for the ensuing drama of no. 8, the recitative in which the valiant Peter cuts off the right ear of the High Priest's servant, which prompts Jesus's statement of his readiness to drink of the cup his father has prepared for him. A second chorale (no. 9) ensues, solid and calming, to be displaced by further accelerated action in the next recitative, which has Jesus arrested and led, bound, before the authorities.

The first aria in the passion is for alto, accompanied by two obbligato oboes and continuo. The text, "Von den Stricken meiner Sünden" (From the tangle of my sins), dwells on the notion that Christ became bound so as to unbind mankind. Sinning, suffering humanity, grieving for Christ's suffering, is frequently represented by the alto voice; the soprano is more likely to represent the soul (as in numerous soprano–bass duets depicting the dialogue between Christ and the soul). The present aria has the feeling of a da capo structure, ABA in form. However, the second A section is not identical to the first, although it recapitulates the text exactly. The aria is in D minor and in triple time. We have earlier met the hemiola (the shifting from three-beat to two-beat melody and back again), and there are many examples of the hemiola in this aria.

After a brief recitative, directing the focus to the forthcoming drama of Peter, we do have a soprano aria perhaps bearing out the suggestion just made about the role of the soprano voice in the passions. This aria has a cheerful, onward-moving flute obbligato and is in the key of B-flat, the key chosen by Bach for the sprightly soprano–bass duet that comes at the end of Cantata BWV 140 (*Wachet auf*), "Mein Freund ist mein, und ich bin dein." The implication of fidelity in the present aria is of course ironic. Following Christ wherever his steps lead is precisely not what Peter is about to do in his dramatic threefold denial of his master. As before, the aria is in triple time, with the additional complications of hemiolas, and is in ABA format, while not being strictly ca capo.

In the recitative immediately following this aria, Peter denies his Lord for the first time. Peter's denial is considerably less fleshed out in John's Gospel than in Matthew's. In the *St. Matthew Passion*, Bach highlights the prophetic words of Jesus at the Last Supper, when Peter asserts that whatever others might do, he for one will never desert his Lord. Jesus's well-known words "Before the cock crows in the morning, you will have denied me three times" are not found in the Gospel passages from John that Bach used. In spite of this, musically speaking, the denial of Peter is much more thoroughly and dramatically portrayed in the *St. John Passion* than in the *St. Matthew*. The second and third denials are treated in the long recitative with chorus interjections, which may be heard as CD Track 9.

Recitative (Evangelist, Peter, Servant), "Und Hannas sandte ihn gebunden" (And Annas Sent Him in Chains), with choral interjection (CD Track 9)

Evangelist: Und Hannas sandte ihn gebunden zu dem Hohenpriester Kaiphas. Simon Petrus stund und wärmete sich, da sprachen sie zu ihm:

Chorus: Bist du nicht seiner Jünger einer?

Evangelist: Er leugnete aber und sprach:

Evangelist: And Annas sent him in chains to the high priest Caiaphas. Simon Peter stood and warmed himself, and people said to him:

Chorus: Are you not one of his disciples?

Evangelist: But he denied it and said:

Petrus: Ich bin's nicht.	*Peter*: I am not.
Evangelist: Spricht des Hohenpriesters Knecht' einer, ein Gefreundter des, dem Petrus das Ohr abgehauen hatte:	*Evangelist*: Then one of the high priests' servants, a friend of him whose ear Peter had cut off, said:
Diener: Sahe ich dich nicht im Garten bei ihm?	*Servant*: Didn't I see you with him in the garden?
Evangelist: Da verleugnete Petrus abermal, und alsobald krähete der Hahn. Da gedachte Petrus an die Worte Jesu und ging hinaus und weinete bitterlich.	*Evangelist*: Peter once again denied it immediately the cock crew. Then Peter remembered the words of Jesus. He went outside and wept bitterly.

Jesus is bound and led away to Caiaphas, while Peter continues to warm himself by the fire, with the officers and servants of the High Priest. Bach paints this idea with a curious little four-note decoration (0:16) that comes back later in a striking fashion, as will be seen. As he does so, the assembled company (the same officers and servant, one surmises), ask in chattering fashion, over about twenty seconds, "Are you not one of his disciples?" (0:21–0:43). This chorus is one of only four numbers to which Bach gave an explicit direction as to tempo, marking it "Allegro." Stipulations regarding tempo or phrasing always mean, in Bach, that he desired to be explicit or to call for an unusual performance practice of some kind. The tempo indication must mean, in this case, that he wanted the chorus to be unusually fast.

Peter's second denial is sung over the perfect cadence marking the end of the Evangelist's next phrase, with an air of blunt, insistent denial (0:49). A servant then brings forth an even more precise charge: "Did I not see you in the garden with him?" (1:02–1:03). Peter denies a third time, and immediately the cock crows. Bach's solution to the need for drama here is fascinating. We have the standard perfect cadence (the V chord to the I chord), but the V is now represented by a melodic decoration in the bass line, placed quite high in pitch, and tradition-ally played *tasto solo*—that is, by the bass instruments alone, without chordal accompaniment (1:13–1:15). A huge shift in mood follows, and the Evangelist paints Peter's tears of remorse in two long, elaborate, highly decorative phrases like nothing else in Bach's recitatives anywhere. The corresponding moment in the *St. Matthew Passion*, usually more elaborately realized than the *St. John*, is rather pale by comparison (1:33–2:21). Note the drawn-out chromaticism in the accompaniment, and observe that the scene ends with an ironic revisiting of the "warming" music.

Part 1 is brought to an end by a tenor aria that seems to be in Peter's own voice, followed by a chorale that dwells on Peter's forgetfulness.

Aria (tenor), "Ach, mein Sinn" (Ah, My Mind), with obbligato violins tutti (CD Track 10)

Ach, mein Sinn,	Ah, my mind,
Wo willt du endlich hin,	Where would you go at last;
Wo soll ich mich erquicken?	Where can I be refreshed?
Bleib ich hier,	Shall I stay here,
Oder wünsch ich mir	Or place
Berg und Hügel auf den Rücken?	Hills and mountains far behind me?
Bei der Welt ist gar kein Rat,	In the world there is no help;
Und im Herzen	And in my heart
Stehn die Schmerzen	Remain the sorrows
Meiner Missetat,	For my misdeed,
Weil der Knecht den Herrn verleug- net hat.	By which the servant has denied his Lord.

The aria is curious in seeming to be huge in scale while lasting a comparatively short time. The aria is in F-sharp minor (the key in which the preceding recitative ended), which is quite remote from the G minor in which the passion started. Both the violin obbligato line and the tenor solo line are uncomfortably angular, as can be heard, mirroring the tightly woven chromaticism at the end of the preceding recitative.

St. John Passion, Part 2

Part 2 begins with Jesus being led away, deserted by the future rock of his church (*Petros* = "rock" in Greek), who has denied his Lord three times between evening and morning and takes us through the whole series of dramatic events culminating in the burial of Jesus, following the claiming of the body by Joseph of Arimathea. Here the two passions diverge slightly, with the drama of Joseph's intervention given rather more thematic weight in the *St. Matthew Passion* than in the *St. John Passion.*

Here is the biblical text for Part 2, found in John 19, ff.

> Then they led Jesus from the house of Caiaphas to the praetorium. It was early. They themselves did not enter the praetorium, so that they might not be defiled, but might eat the Passover.
>
> So Pilate went out to them and said, "What accusation do you bring against this man?"
>
> They answered him, "If this man were not an evildoer, we would not have handed him over."
>
> Pilate said to them, "Take him yourselves and judge him by your own law." The Jews said to him, "It is not lawful for us to put any man to death."
>
> This was to fulfil the word which Jesus had spoken to show by what death he was to die.
>
> Pilate entered the praetorium again and called Jesus, and said to him, "Are you the King of the Jews?" Jesus answered, "Do you say this of your own accord, or did others say it to you about me?"
>
> Pilate answered, "Am I a Jew? Your own nation and the chief priests have handed you over to me; what have you done?"
>
> Jesus answered, "My kingship is not of this world; if my kingship were of this world, my servants would fight, that I might not be handed over to the Jews; but my kingship is not from the world."
>
> Pilate said to him, "So you are a king?" Jesus answered, "You say that I am a king. For this I was born, and for this I have come into the world, to bear witness to the truth. Everyone who is of the truth hears my voice."
>
> Pilate said to him, "What is truth?"
>
> After he had said this, he went out to the Jews again, and told them, "I find no crime in him.
>
> "But you have a custom that I should release one man for you at the Passover; will you have me release for you the King of the

Jews?" They cried out again, "Not this man, but Barabbas!" Now Barabbas was a robber.

Then Pilate took Jesus and scourged him.

And the soldiers plaited a crown of thorns, and put it on his head, and arrayed him in a purple robe; they came up to him, saying, "Hail, King of the Jews!" and struck him with their hands.

Pilate went out again, and said to them, "See, I am bringing him out to you, that you may know that I find no crime in him."

So Jesus came out, wearing the crown of thorns and the purple robe. Pilate said to them, "Behold the man!"

When the chief priests and the officers saw him, they cried out, "Crucify him, crucify him!" Pilate said to them, "Take him yourselves and crucify him, for I find no crime in him."

The Jews answered him, "We have a law, and by that law he ought to die, because he has made himself the Son of God."

When Pilate heard these words, he was the more afraid; he entered the praetorium again and said to Jesus, "Where are you from?" But Jesus gave no answer.

Pilate therefore said to him, "You will not speak to me? Do you not know that I have power to release you, and power to crucify you?"

Jesus answered him, "You would have no power over me unless it had been given you from above; therefore he who delivered me to you has the greater sin."

Upon this Pilate sought to release him, but the Jews cried out, "If you release this man, you are not Caesar's friend; every one who makes himself a king sets himself against Caesar."

When Pilate heard these words, he brought Jesus out and sat down on the judgment seat at a place called The Pavement, and in Hebrew, Gab'batha.

Now it was the day of Preparation of the Passover; it was about the sixth hour. He said to the Jews, "Behold your King!"

They cried out, "Away with him, away with him, crucify him!" Pilate said to them, "Shall I crucify your King?" The chief priests answered, "We have no king but Caesar."

Then he handed him over to them to be crucified.

So they took Jesus, and he went out, bearing his own cross, to the place called the place of a skull, which is called in Hebrew Golgotha.

There they crucified him, and with him two others, one on either side, and Jesus between them.

Pilate also wrote a title and put it on the cross; it read, "Jesus of Nazareth, the King of the Jews."

Many of the Jews read this title, for the place where Jesus was crucified was near the city; and it was written in Hebrew, in Latin, and in Greek.

The chief priests of the Jews then said to Pilate, "Do not write, 'The King of the Jews,' but, 'This man said, I am King of the Jews.'"

Pilate answered, "What I have written I have written."

When the soldiers had crucified Jesus they took his garments and made four parts, one for each soldier; also his tunic. But the tunic was without seam, woven from top to bottom; so they said to one another, "Let us not tear it, but cast lots for it to see whose it shall be." This was to fulfil the scripture, "They parted my garments among them, and for my clothing they cast lots."

So the soldiers did this. But standing by the cross of Jesus were his mother, and his mother's sister, Mary the wife of Clopas, and Mary Magdalene.

When Jesus saw his mother, and the disciple whom he loved standing near, he said to his mother, "Woman, behold, your son!"

Then he said to the disciple, "Behold, your mother!" And from that hour the disciple took her to his own home.

After this Jesus, knowing that all was now finished, said (to fulfil the scripture), "I thirst."

A bowl full of vinegar stood there; so they put a sponge full of the vinegar on hyssop and held it to his mouth. When Jesus had received the vinegar, he said, "It is finished"; and he bowed his head and gave up his spirit.

Since it was the day of Preparation, in order to prevent the bodies from remaining on the cross on the sabbath (for that sabbath was a high day), the Jews asked Pilate that their legs might be broken, and that they might be taken away.

So the soldiers came and broke the legs of the first, and of the other who had been crucified with him; but when they came to Jesus and saw that he was already dead, they did not break his legs.

But one of the soldiers pierced his side with a spear, and at once there came out blood and water.

He who saw it has borne witness—his testimony is true, and he knows that he tells the truth—that you also may believe.

For these things took place that the scripture might be fulfilled, "Not a bone of him shall be broken."

And again another scripture says, "They shall look on him whom they have pierced."

After this Joseph of Arimathea, who was a disciple of Jesus, but secretly, for fear of the Jews, asked Pilate that he might take away the body of Jesus, and Pilate gave him leave. So he came and took away his body.

Nicodemus also, who had at first come to him by night, came bringing a mixture of myrrh and aloes, about a hundred pounds' weight.

They took the body of Jesus, and bound it in linen cloths with the spices, as is the burial custom of the Jews.

Now in the place where he was crucified there was a garden, and in the garden a new tomb where no one had ever been laid.

So because of the Jewish day of Preparation, as the tomb was close at hand, they laid Jesus there.

St. John Passion, Part 2: Commentary

Part 2 of the *Passion* is much longer than Part 1, is on a much higher plane of intensity, and makes for demanding listening. As they followed on from the sermon, Bach's audience would have known that several intensely human dramas within the bigger narrative awaited them— those of Pilate, Barabbas, and above all the fickleness of the crowd being some of the most prominent.

Unlike Part 1, Part 2 opens with a chorale that foreshadows the nighttime arrest and the ensuing, trial, conviction, and execution. The first recitative leads directly into the drama of Pilate. He asks the crowd what specific charges they bring against Jesus. Their answer, given in a furious fugal chorus, is tautologous in the extreme: "If he were not a sinner, we would not have brought him before you" (no. 23). Note in the chorus the rising chromatic phrase with which the word *Übeltäter* (malefactor) is painted. Falling chromatic sequences are quite common in Bach, rising figures much less so. This is but the first of a series of choruses of mounting ferocity and sarcastic contempt: no. 25 has the crowd wanting Jesus's blood but unwilling to shed it themselves, and seeking to establish Pilate as their proxy; in no. 29, invited to choose a pardon for Jesus or the robber Barabbas, they choose the latter; in no. 34, following the ironic clothing of Jesus in a purple robe, they hail him in cheerful B-flat, the King of the Jews, with chirruping oboes and flutes; no. 36 shows the crowd's true feelings, as they cry, "Kreuzige" (crucify), one word described in twenty-two measures of fugal writing, full of unprepared discords and chromatic twisting and turning; no. 38 invokes the law in attempted vindication; no. 42 charges Pilate with disloyalty to Caesar if he lets Jesus go; no. 44 returns to atavistic bloodlust, rather in the manner of no. 36; and no. 46 has the crowd swearing loyalty to Caesar. The drama of the crowd is one angle; that of Pilate another. One moment to listen for is in no. 30, a recitative in which Jesus is scourged by Pilate, described by the Evangelist in a florid passage lasting almost ten seconds and consisting of fifty-six notes leading from middle A-flat (a sixth above middle C) to tenor D (a seventh below middle C). There are so many other treasures in these pages, such as a meditative bass arioso (midway between recitative and aria), accompanied by two violas d'amore, lute obbligato, and continuo. The viola pair is retained in a tenor aria that immediately follows the arioso and lasts more than seven minutes, making it the longest number in the entire work. If we heed the unusual tempo indication for the arioso (Bach marked it "adagio," seemingly redundantly, for any good performer's instinct would be to play the piece slowly), the arioso and aria taken together would last almost nine minutes, as indeed is the case in Bach Collegium Japan's performance. Finally, listen in these pages for two especially beautiful chorales, calling even more deeply upon the expressive range of the chorus. If you have the opportunity to listen to the whole sequence of recitatives, choruses, and arias, do so; attempt to visualize the scene in Leipzig as the townsfolk performers acted out this spectacle of contempt, selfishness, and cruelty for their neighbors. Perhaps the most dramatic moment of all is when the chorus, having hurled the final, almost inarticulate "Weg mit dem, weg mit dem" (Away with him, away with him), suddenly become the faithful again, seeking to follow Jesus to his suffering in an ironic reversal of Peter's earlier desertion in no. 48, discussion of which follows.

Aria (bass), "Eilt, ihr angefochtnen Seelen" (Haste, You Tempted Spirits), with choral interjections (CD Track 11)

Eilt, ihr angefochtnen Seelen,	Haste, you tempted spirits,
Geht aus euren Marterhöhlen,	Leave the caverns of your torture,
Eilt—Wohin?—nach Golgatha!	Haste—Where to?—to Golgatha!
Nehmet an des Glaubens Flügel,	Put on the wings of faith,
Flieht—Wohin?—zum	Flee—Where to?—to the hill of
Kreuzeshügel,	the cross,
Eure Wohlfahrt blüht allda!	For your welfare is flowering there!

The aria is for bass soloist, accompanied by tutti strings. It is in triple time, is in the opening key of the whole work (G minor), and is characterized by rapid runs, in sixteenth-notes and angular skips. Of course one expects and finds hemiola patterns throughout, but nowhere more startlingly so than in the chorus interruptions, with the repeated word "Wohin?" (Where?). Tutti strings begin the running, to be echoed by continuo after a couple of measures (0:00–0:03). The instrumental introduction ends with a passage of hemiolas (1:15–1:19), and the soloist enters. Nothing in Bach calls for more vocal control than the next measures, describing the haste with which the faithful must follow. At 0:54 the chorus enters with its question (or some of the chorus—the basses are silent, presumably to avoid swamping the bass soloist, who remains active while the chorus sings). The biggest surprise is in the answer to the question: "nach Golgotha," "to Golgotha," sung on the tritone, the devil's interval, which we encountered earlier. The first section ends with a fermata (in Bach's own hand) from the chorus. A middle (B) section follows, slightly milder in feel (2:05ff), in a related major key (E-flat). The theme now is not haste, but waiting, and Bach paints this with a B-flat sustained over two measures by the soloist. Before long we return to the first material (2:28), another fermata from the chorus (3:24–3:26), one last definitive response from the soloist, and a reprise of the opening instrumental material.

Preparations for the crucifixion ensue, including the highly dramatic moment when the chorus now takes on the role of the soldiers, who in a long and calculatedly ugly fugue decide to cast lots for Jesus's robe rather than tear it up among them (no. 54).

For some, the high point of the passion is the aria in which the alto soloist, playing the role of the faithful bystander, picks up the last words of Jesus, "Es ist vollbracht" (It is finished).

Aria (alto), "Es ist vollbracht" (It Is Fulfilled) (CD Track 12)

Es ist vollbracht!	It is fulfilled!
O Trost vor die gekränkten Seelen!	O hope for the sick spirit!
Die Trauernacht	The night of grief
Läßt nun die letzte Stunde zählen.	Is now counting the last hours.
Der Held aus Juda siegt mit Macht	The hero of Judah wins with might
Und schließt den Kampf.	And ends the battle.
Es ist vollbracht!	It is fulfilled!

For the third time, Bach gives a specific tempo direction at the start of this aria. He marks it *molto adagio*—very slow. He must mean very, very slow. The tempo on our recording seems just right. The aria is for alto (male alto, of course, in Bach's time); the vocal range called for is great—from tenor B (half a step below middle C) to treble D (a ninth above middle C). The line returns again and again to this high point. Even allowing for the fact that pitch in Bach's time may have been about half a step below today's concert pitch (A = 419 as opposed to A = 440), this is still very high. This aria is considered to be absolutely one of the high points of the alto repertoire, and there are many fine recordings of it, notably those of Dame Janet Baker (contralto) and the English countertenor David Daniels. The present Bach Collegium Japan performance features the phenomenal Yoshikazu Mera and really could not be bettered. Mera's performance lasts over six minutes yet never drags. (There exists another, earlier recording by Mera in which he spins the piece out to over seven minutes.)

The accompaniment is for continuo and viola da gamba obbligato, and the aria holds as key a place in the gamba repertoire as it does in the alto. For the technically minded, it may be interesting to know that Bach in the manuscript wrote certain decorative "grace" notes in unprecedentedly small handwriting, and this has led performers to suppose that these notes should be even shorter or more delicate—or both—than usual. This is the practice followed on our recording and may be clearly heard at 0:05, 0:08, and 0:12. The vocal line is marked in just the same way (0:59, 1:22). The aria is in B minor, which seems to have been a special key for Bach—the key of the great mass—as part of its glory is that it is so closely related to D major, the trumpet key, the key of rejoicing. This is where the alto voice leads us to at the end of its first long phrases (2:01). The viola da gamba then takes us, in one long phrase, a step toward the "flatter" key of G major, flatter, and seemingly more wearisome, as the text indicates. The vocal line resumes and soon settles on a long—extremely long—low C-sharp (2:48), held for almost fifteen seconds. Soon the soloist finds his way to F-sharp minor, the dominant key of B minor, which is much as we would expect (3:40). Then—always expect the unexpected—the gamba takes the action to D major, and we discover what Bach's intentions were all along (3:44–4:09). We have been brought to the martial key of D major and to an astonishing shift in tempo. Bach actually marks this section *Alla breve*, essentially, one-in-a-bar, and the text is heroic—"Der Held aus Juda siegt mit Macht" (The hero of Juda wins with might). The vocal line here is demanding in the extreme, especially around 4:44, where a long passage of sixteenth-notes calls for wide skips. In singing at high speed, stepwise melodic patterns are relatively straightforward, skipwise not at all so. But the struggle depicted here ends with victory in death, as the furious music comes to a pause over another devil's chord (4:50–4:53) and the soloist returns to the original idea (4:55). The gamba has a reprise of the introductory material. Then comes the greatest surprise of all—at the final cadence, the soloist restates the original idea (5:52), with a final grace note, on the last downbeat, a plangent discord, C-sharp to B.

The Evangelist resumes, to confirm what we suspect that harsh C-sharp was about: "Und neigte das Haupt, und verschied" (He bowed his head and was gone). This recitative flows directly into a wonderful bass aria, the tempo also marked deliberately by Bach as "Adagio," in compound, 12/8 time—a slow dance. The text is a question: since you are crucified, and since in your words it is fulfilled, will all the world be redeemed? The answer is a while in coming but, when it does come, is a fourfold "Ja" (Yes). The aria is essentially a chorale fantasia; slowly and quietly the chorus sings the same chorale melody we first heard at the end of Part 1, directly after the denial of Peter. The drama continues with two recitatives in which the air of peace we experience at the end of this aria is shattered by furious scales, tremblings, and rumblings, as the Evangelist depicts the upheaval in the heavens that is said to have followed the death of Jesus.

The final chorus of the *St. John Passion* is a steadily moving funeral ode, in C minor, in triple time, and in ABA format. The B section is often sung by soloists or a semichorus of soprano, alto, and tenor—no bass, thus perhaps echoing the Golgotha aria.

St. Matthew Passion

rand as the *St. John Passion* is, it is somewhat dwarfed by its younger sibling the *St. Matthew Passion*, first performed in 1727 and revised to its present definitive form in 1736. First, the *St. Matthew* is united through its libretto in a way the *St. John Passion* could not be. The libretto text is from one author, Picander, with whom Bach is known to have collaborated closely; that of the *St. John* was assembled from the work of a variety of authors. Second, the scale of the *St. Matthew* is huge, in conception and in forces. The choral music, for instance, is conceived for double choir, each with its own separate continuo group, and a capable double orchestra, and there is indeed, in the final revision, a third choral force, that of the boy soprano unison choir, supported by organ, that appears in a number of places, most strikingly in the opening number, where it holds the cantus firmus chorale "O Lamm Gottes unschuldig" (O Lamb of God Unspotted), making nine choral lines. The double choir supports an allegorical intention of the librettist Picander, who conceived of a dialogue between the daughters of Zion and the faithful—a distinction more or less lost on the modern listener but that the more literate of Bach's original audience may well have grasped. Among many other daring musical inventions is the use of instrumental accompaniment in the recitatives (violins 1 and 2, viola, continuo) for the words of Jesus, except for his dying words, when the ensemble deserts him. The oratorio lasts almost half as long again as the *St. John Passion*, nearly three hours. Perhaps it is not so surprising the *St. Matthew Passion* was to be Bach's last major composition for the Leipzig congregations. The passion was performed three or perhaps four times—once or twice in 1727, once in 1736, and once again toward the end of Bach's life, in the 1740s.

We have a clue to Bach's estimation of his own work in the autograph manuscript, unusually carefully prepared even for him. Wolff (2000, 298) describes the mutlicolored text (red for the Gospel language and for the cantus firmus chorale just mentioned). At some point the opening pages of this fair copy were damaged, and Bach repaired it carefully, pasting on strips of paper and replacing some lost sections. He also wrote out a complete new set of performing parts. The oratorio text operates on three levels: Picander's libretto; a large number of chorales, most set quite simply in a form the congregation would have been familiar with; and the biblical text, which is drawn from chapters 26 and 27 of the Gospel according to St. Matthew, the text of which follows. Bach does not follow the text sequence as closely as he had in the *St. John*, and so the text is now given in the King James Version of the Bible without comment, as the backdrop to the musical work. Listeners would be well served to follow the whole work with a copy of the vocal score. One basic distinction to watch for is that in the *St. Matthew Passion*, Peter's denial of Christ (described toward the end of the very long chapter 26) does not come until well into Part 2; in the *St. John* it provided a dramatic ending to Part 1. In the *St. Matthew Passion*, this role is played by the drama of Judas.

Gospel According to St. Matthew

Chapter 26

And it came to pass, when Jesus had finished all these sayings, he said unto his disciples,

Ye know that after two days is the feast of the passover, and the Son of man is betrayed to be crucified.

Then assembled together the chief priests, and the scribes, and the elders of the people, unto the palace of the high priest, who was called Caiaphas,

And consulted that they might take Jesus by subtilty, and kill him.

But they said, Not on the feast day, lest there be an uproar among the people.

Now when Jesus was in Bethany, in the house of Simon the leper,

There came unto him a woman having an alabaster box of very precious ointment, and poured it on his head, as he sat at meat.

But when his disciples saw it, they had indignation, saying, To what purpose is this waste?

For this ointment might have been sold for much, and given to the poor.

When Jesus understood it, he said unto them, Why trouble ye the woman? for she hath wrought a good work upon me.

For ye have the poor always with you; but me ye have not always. For in that she hath poured this ointment on my body, she did it for my burial.

Verily I say unto you, Wheresoever this gospel shall be preached in the whole world, there shall also this, that this woman hath done, be told for a memorial of her.

Then one of the twelve, called Judas Iscariot, went unto the chief priests,

And said unto them, What will ye give me, and I will deliver him unto you? And they covenanted with him for thirty pieces of silver.

And from that time he sought opportunity to betray him.

Now the first day of the feast of unleavened bread the disciples came to Jesus, saying unto him, Where wilt thou that we prepare for thee to eat the passover?

And he said, Go into the city to such a man, and say unto him, The Master saith, My time is at hand; I will keep the passover at thy house with my disciples.

And the disciples did as Jesus had appointed them; and they made ready the passover.

Now when the even was come, he sat down with the twelve.

And as they did eat, he said, Verily I say unto you, that one of you shall betray me.

And they were exceeding sorrowful, and began every one of them to say unto him, Lord, is it I?

And he answered and said, He that dippeth his hand with me in the dish, the same shall betray me. The Son of man goeth as it is written of him: but woe unto that man by whom the Son of man is betrayed! it had been good for that man if he had not been born.

Then Judas, which betrayed him, answered and said, Master, is it I? He said unto him, Thou hast said.

And as they were eating, Jesus took bread, and blessed it, and brake it, and gave it to the disciples, and said, Take, eat; this is my body.

And he took the cup, and gave thanks, and gave it to them, saying, Drink ye all of it;

For this is my blood of the new testament, which is shed for many for the remission of sins.

But I say unto you, I will not drink henceforth of this fruit of the vine, until that day when I drink it new with you in my Father's kingdom.

And when they had sung an hymn, they went out into the mount of Olives.

Then saith Jesus unto them, All ye shall be offended because of me this night: for it is written, I will smite the shepherd, and the sheep of the flock shall be scattered abroad.

But after I am risen again, I will go before you into Galilee.

Peter answered and said unto him, Though all men shall be offended because of thee, yet will I never be offended.

Jesus said unto him, Verily I say unto thee, That this night, before the cock crow, thou shalt deny me thrice.

Peter said unto him, Though I should die with thee, yet will I not deny thee. Likewise also said all the disciples.

Then cometh Jesus with them unto a place called Gethsemane, and saith unto the disciples, Sit ye here, while I go and pray yonder.

And he took with him Peter and the two sons of Zebedee, and began to be sorrowful and very heavy.

Then saith he unto them, My soul is exceeding sorrowful, even unto death: tarry ye here, and watch with me.

And he went a little farther, and fell on his face, and prayed, saying, O my Father, if it be possible, let this cup pass from me: nevertheless not as I will, but as thou wilt.

And he cometh unto the disciples, and findeth them asleep, and saith unto Peter, What, could ye not watch with me one hour?

Watch and pray, that ye enter not into temptation: the spirit indeed is willing, but the flesh is weak.

He went away again the second time, and prayed, saying, O my Father, if this cup may not pass away from me, except I drink it, thy will be done.

And he came and found them asleep again: for their eyes were heavy. And he left them, and went away again, and prayed the third time, saying the same words.

Then cometh he to his disciples, and saith unto them, Sleep on now, and take your rest: behold, the hour is at hand, and the Son of man is betrayed into the hands of sinners.

Rise, let us be going: behold, he is at hand that doth betray me. And while he yet spake, lo, Judas, one of the twelve, came, and with him a great multitude with swords and staves, from the chief priests and elders of the people.

Now he that betrayed him gave them a sign, saying, Whomsoever I shall kiss, that same is he: hold him fast.

And forthwith he came to Jesus, and said, Hail, master; and kissed him. And Jesus said unto him, Friend, wherefore art thou come?

Then came they, and laid hands on Jesus and took him. And, behold, one of them which were with Jesus stretched out his hand, and drew his sword, and struck a servant of the high priest's, and smote off his ear.

Then said Jesus unto him, Put up again thy sword into his place: for all they that take the sword shall perish with the sword.

Thinkest thou that I cannot now pray to my Father, and he shall presently give me more than twelve legions of angels?

But how then shall the scriptures be fulfilled, that thus it must be?

In that same hour said Jesus to the multitudes, Are ye come out as against a thief with swords and staves for to take me? I sat daily with you teaching in the temple, and ye laid no hold on me.

But all this was done, that the scriptures of the prophets might be fulfilled. Then all the disciples forsook him, and fled.

And they that had laid hold on Jesus led him away to Caiaphas the high priest, where the scribes and the elders were assembled.

But Peter followed him afar off unto the high priest's palace, and went in, and sat with the servants, to see the end.

Now the chief priests, and elders, and all the council, sought false witness against Jesus, to put him to death;

But found none: yea, though many false witnesses came, yet found they none. At the last came two false witnesses,

And said, This fellow said, I am able to destroy the temple of God, and to build it in three days.

And the high priest arose, and said unto him, Answerest thou nothing? what is it which these witness against thee?

But Jesus held his peace, And the high priest answered and said unto him, I adjure thee by the living God, that thou tell us whether thou be the Christ, the Son of God.

Jesus saith unto him, Thou hast said: nevertheless I say unto you, Hereafter shall ye see the Son of man sitting on the right hand of power, and coming in the clouds of heaven.

Then the high priest rent his clothes, saying, He hath spoken blasphemy; what further need have we of witnesses? behold, now ye have heard his blasphemy.

What think ye? They answered and said, He is guilty of death. Then did they spit in his face, and buffeted him; and others smote him with the palms of their hands,

Saying, Prophesy unto us, thou Christ, Who is he that smote thee?

Now Peter sat without in the palace: and a damsel came unto him, saying, Thou also wast with Jesus of Galilee.

But he denied before them all, saying, I know not what thou sayest.

And when he was gone out into the porch, another maid saw him, and said unto them that were there, This fellow was also with Jesus of Nazareth.

And again he denied with an oath, I do not know the man. And after a while came unto him they that stood by, and said to Peter, Surely thou also art one of them; for thy speech bewrayeth thee.

Then began he to curse and to swear, saying, I know not the man. And immediately the cock crew.

And Peter remembered the word of Jesus, which said unto him, Before the cock crow, thou shalt deny me thrice. And he went out, and wept bitterly.

Chapter 27

When the morning was come, all the chief priests and elders of the people took counsel against Jesus to put him to death:

And when they had bound him, they led him away, and delivered him to Pontius Pilate the governor.

Then Judas, which had betrayed him, when he saw that he was condemned, repented himself, and brought again the thirty pieces of silver to the chief priests and elders,

Saying, I have sinned in that I have betrayed the innocent blood. And they said, What is that to us? see thou to that.

And he cast down the pieces of silver in the temple, and departed, and went and hanged himself.

And the chief priests took the silver pieces, and said, It is not lawful for to put them into the treasury, because it is the price of blood.

And they took counsel, and bought with them the potter's field, to bury strangers in.

Wherefore that field was called, The field of blood, unto this day.

Then was fulfilled that which was spoken by Jeremy the prophet, saying, And they took the thirty pieces of silver, the price of him that was valued, whom they of the children of Israel did value;

And gave them for the potter's field, as the Lord appointed me.

And Jesus stood before the governor: and the governor asked him, saying, Art thou the King of the Jews? And Jesus said unto him, Thou sayest.

And when he was accused of the chief priests and elders, he answered nothing.

Then said Pilate unto him, Hearest thou not how many things they witness against thee?

And he answered him to never a word; insomuch that the governor marvelled greatly.

Now at that feast the governor was wont to release unto the people a prisoner, whom they would.

And they had then a notable prisoner, called Barabbas.

Therefore when they were gathered together, Pilate said unto them, Whom will ye that I release unto you? Barabbas, or Jesus which is called Christ?

For he knew that for envy they had delivered him.

When he was set down on the judgment seat, his wife sent unto him, saying, Have thou nothing to do with that just man: for I have suffered many things this day in a dream because of him.

But the chief priests and elders persuaded the multitude that they should ask Barabbas, and destroy Jesus.

The governor answered and said unto them, Whether of the twain will ye that I release unto you? They said, Barabbas.

Pilate saith unto them, What shall I do then with Jesus which is called Christ? They all say unto him, Let him be crucified.

And the governor said, Why, what evil hath he done? But they cried out the more, saying, Let him be crucified.

When Pilate saw that he could prevail nothing, but that rather a tumult was made, he took water, and washed his hands before the multitude, saying, I am innocent of the blood of this just person: see ye to it.

Then answered all the people, and said, His blood be on us, and on our children.

Then released he Barabbas unto them: and when he had scourged Jesus, he delivered him to be crucified.

Then the soldiers of the governor took Jesus into the common hall, and gathered unto him the whole band of soldiers.

And they stripped him, and put on him a scarlet robe.

And when they had platted a crown of thorns, they put it upon his head, and a reed in his right hand: and they bowed the knee before him, and mocked him, saying, Hail, King of the Jews!

And they spit upon him, and took the reed, and smote him on the head.

And after that they had mocked him, they took the robe off from him, and put his own raiment on him, and led him away to crucify him.

And as they came out, they found a man of Cyrene, Simon by name: him they compelled to bear his cross.

And when they were come unto a place called Golgotha, that is to say, a place of a skull,

They gave him vinegar to drink mingled with gall: and when he had tasted thereof, he would not drink.

And they crucified him, and parted his garments, casting lots: that it might be fulfilled which was spoken by the prophet, They parted my garments among them, and upon my vesture did they cast lots.

And sitting down they watched him there; And set up over his head his accusation written,

THIS IS JESUS THE KING OF THE JEWS.

Then were there two thieves crucified with him, one on the right hand, and another on the left.

And they that passed by reviled him, wagging their heads,

And saying, Thou that destroyest the temple, and buildest it in three days, save thyself. If thou be the Son of God, come down from the cross.

Likewise also the chief priests mocking him, with the scribes and elders, said,

He saved others; himself he cannot save. If he be the King of Israel, let him now come down from the cross, and we will believe him.

He trusted in God; let him deliver him now, if he will have him: for he said, I am the Son of God.

The thieves also, which were crucified with him, cast the same in his teeth.

Now from the sixth hour there was darkness over all the land unto the ninth hour.

And about the ninth hour Jesus cried with a loud voice, saying, Eli, Eli, lama sabachthani? that is to say, My God, my God, why hast thou forsaken me?

Some of them that stood there, when they heard that, said, This man calleth for Elias.

And straightway one of them ran, and took a spunge, and filled it with vinegar, and put it on a reed, and gave him to drink.

The rest said, Let be, let us see whether Elias will come to save him.

Jesus, when he had cried again with a loud voice, yielded up the ghost.

And, behold, the veil of the temple was rent in twain from the top to the bottom; and the earth did quake, and the rocks rent;

And the graves were opened; and many bodies of the saints which slept arose,

And came out of the graves after his resurrection, and went into the holy city, and appeared unto many.

Now when the centurion, and they that were with him, watching Jesus, saw the earthquake, and those things that were done, they feared greatly, saying, Truly this was the Son of God.

And many women were there beholding afar off, which followed Jesus from Galilee, ministering unto him:

Among which was Mary Magdalene, and Mary the mother of James and Joses, and the mother of Zebedee's children.

When the even was come, there came a rich man of Arimathaea, named Joseph, who also himself was Jesus's disciple:

He went to Pilate, and begged the body of Jesus. Then Pilate commanded the body to be delivered.

And when Joseph had taken the body, he wrapped it in a clean linen cloth,

And laid it in his own new tomb, which he had hewn out in the rock: and he rolled a great stone to the door of the sepulchre, and departed.

And there was Mary Magdalene, and the other Mary, sitting over against the sepulchre.

Now the next day, that followed the day of the preparation, the chief priests and Pharisees came together unto Pilate,

Saying, Sir, we remember that that deceiver said, while he was yet alive, After three days I will rise again.

Command therefore that the sepulchre be made sure until the third day, lest his disciples come by night, and steal him away, and say unto the people, He is risen from the dead: so the last error shall be worse than the first.

Pilate said unto them, Ye have a watch: go your way, make it as sure as ye can.

So they went, and made the sepulchre sure, sealing the stone, and setting a watch.

Listeners' guide to the *St. Matthew Passion*

Chorus, "Kommt, ihr Töchter, helft mir klagen" (Come, You Daughters, Help Me Mourn), with cantus firmus chorale "O Lamm Gottes unschuldig" (O Lamb of God Unspotted)
(CD Track 13)

The opening chorus is for double choir, which are used *antiphonally* (as balanced, separate choirs, in dialogue).

Kommt, ihr Töchter, helft mir klagen,	Come, daughters, help me mourn!
Sehet! Wen?	Look! At whom?
Den Bräutigam.	The Bridegroom!
Seht ihn! Wie?	Look at him! How does he come?
Als wie ein Lamm.	Like a lamb.

Kommt, ihr Töchter, helft mir klagen,	Come, daughters, help me mourn,
Sehet! Was?	Look! At what?
Seht die Geduld.	Look at his patience.
Seht! Wohin?	Look! Where?
Auf unsre Schuld.	At our guilt.
Sehet ihn aus Lieb und Huld	Look at him carrying, out of love and grace,
Holz zum Kreuze selber tragen.	wood for the cross himself.

Alongside these eight vocal lines there is a ninth, a choir of boys' voices that sing this chorale:

O Lamm Gottes, unschuldig,	O Lamb of God unspotted!
am Stamm des Kreuzes geschlachtet,	You are slaughtered on the cross,
Allzeit erfund'n geduldig,	Always patient and humble,
Wie wohl du warest verachtet;	Though scorned and humiliated.
All Sünd hast du getragen,	You have taken all sins upon yourself,
sonst müssten wir verzagen.	Without which we would have no hope:
Erbarm dich unser, O Jesu!	Have mercy on us, Jesus.

The boys begin this chorale in response to the depiction of Christ as the Bridegroom who is also a sacrificial lamb.

The chorus is in E minor (in some ways a cooler key emotionally than the tormented G minor of *St. John Passion* Part 1), and instead of the febrile sixteenth-notes we have compound meter—in 12/8 time, with four pulses to the measure with underlying triplets, rather in the manner of a siciliano, a dance form popular in Bach's time, a sort of slow jig, often with a pastoral feel. Compare the pastoral music of the *Christmas Oratorio* and the aria "He Shall Feed His Flock Like a Shepherd," in Handel's *Messiah*. The two orchestras are together at the start of the movement, though they, too, come to be used antiphonally as the piece goes on. Under the lilting rhythms is a *pedal point*; the continuo line holds on to the low E tonic note for five full measures before starting, at 0:30 to climb upward, stepwise from low E to middle C (a motif taken up later by the basses in the chorus, at 2:01ff). There is a second pedal point, also of five measures, but this time on the dominant note of B (0:46–1:13). The chorus enters—both choirs together for now—at 1:29 with the opening words "Kommt, ihr Töchter" (Come, You Daughters, Help Me Mourn). There are unasked, unanswered questions at this point: Come where? Why? Whom to see? They are soon asked, and answered, for the choirs divide at 2:19. Choir 1 sings, "Sehet" (See), and their opposite numbers reply, "Wen . . . wie . . . wen . . . wie?" (Whom? How? Whom? How?) (2:19, 2:24, 2:29, 2:35). The answers are: (See whom?) See the bridegroom; and (How?) As a lamb. This is the thought that triggers the chorale (2:39) that the boys sing as a long cantus firmus (in four-time) while the choirs, united now, weave around in twelve-time, in a somewhat undifferentiated manner for a while. But at the second phrase of the chorale (3:00), the choirs divide again and return to the question-and-answer material such as we have just heard. This first section of the movement comes to rest in the relative-major key of G, and the continuo line sets off on the familiar climbing scale passage, to lead us back toward the home key, for a reprise of the opening lines of the chorale melody (lines 3 and 4 of the text). The chorale entries are at 3:51 and 4:12, after which we are headed to the middle section of the movement, and new material.

We have several measures of orchestral ritornello, situated on a G major pedal point, before the choirs divide again, one urging, "Seht" (See!), and the second choir responding with a light, rather detached, "Wohin?" (Where?) (5:02), the orchestras also in antiphonal groups with a graceful set of sixteenth-note dialogues, before the cantus firmus returns at 5:23 and 5:51. The choirs unite at the end of this last entry in a conclusive-sounding passage of block harmony (6:05). The impending end of the chorus is further underlined by a striking bass line at 7:00 descending in half-notes. The air of conclusion is confirmed at 7:09 with a last five-measure dominant (B) pedal point (7:09ff), and the chorus ends with, remarkably, no final orchestral ritornello.

The following recitative (no. 2) features the first of Jesus's statements, clad in what many listeners feel to be a kind of halo of sustained strings. In these words Jesus refers to prophecies of his impending crucifixion, in what is known as a *melisma* (one syllable sung to a series of notes), in this case a highly chromatic one, with, as one might expect, the harmonic underpinnings of the Neapolitan sixth, or devil's chord. The shift between the *recitativo secco* ("dry" recitative, accompanied only by continuo) of the Evangelist and the *recitativo accompagnato* or *arioso* is a striking characteristic of the *St. Matthew Passion*, and we hear it again shortly. First, though, we have the first of many chorales (no. 3), a recitative (no. 4A) in which Caiaphas, the high priest, rather prematurely introduces the notion of a crucifixion, and the first dramatic chorus (in double choir), in which the high priest's counselors object, on the grounds that it might create an uproar. The chorus has to make a quick change of musical wardrobe, as it were, to portray the disciples, who object to the cost of the precious ointment used by a faithful woman to anoint Jesus's head while he is staying with Simon the leper (no. 4D). Then comes the wonderful passage of accompanied recitative (no. 4E) in which Jesus immortalizes the woman's deeds. This is turn gives way to an arioso, and then a da capo aria for alto, accompanied by two flutes and continuo, the voice of the faithful asking to be permitted to anoint Jesus, explicitly for burial, as did the poor woman just featured in the action.

The positive flavor of these first numbers is dispelled by the entry into the action of Judas, Jesus's betrayer, first heard in the recitative no. 7, and this is followed by a soprano aria (marked "Soprano chori II" by Bach, and therefore one of the chorus of the faithful. This is a da capo aria, and the B section graphically depicts the serpent bosom of the betrayer.

The action moves toward the Last Supper, the identification by Jesus of his betrayer, and the institution of the Eucharist.

Recitative (Evangelist, Judas, Jesus), "Er antwortete und sprach" (He Answered and Said) (CD Track 14)

Evangelist: Er antwortete und sprach:

Evangelist: He answered and said:

Jesus: Der mit der Hand mit mir in die Schüssel tauchet der wird mich verraten. Des Menschen Sohn gehet zwar dahin, wie von ihm geschrieben stehet; doch wehe dem Menschen, durch welchen des Menschen Sohn verraten wird! Es wäre ihm besser, dass derselbiche Mensch noch geboren wäre.

Jesus: One who dips his hand with me in this dish this evening will betray me. The Son of Man goes on his way, as has been written. But woe to him by whom the Son of Man will be betrayed. For him it were better if he had never been born.

Evangelist: Da antwortete Judas, der ihn verriet, und sprach:

Evangelist: Then answered Judas, who betrayed him, and said:

Judas: Bin ich's, Rabbi?

Judas: Is it I, Lord?

Evangelist: Er sprach zu ihm:

Evangelist: He said to him:

Jesus: Du sagest's.

Jesus: As you say.

Evangelist: Da sie aber assen, nahm Jesus das Brot, dankete und brach's und gab's den Jüngern und sprach:

Evangelist: As they were eating, he took the bread, blessed it and broke it up, gave it to the disciples, and said:

Jesus: Nehmet, esset, das ist mein Leib.

Jesus: Take and eat. This is my body.

Evangelist: Und er nahm den Kelch und dankete, gab ihnen den und sprach:

Evangelist: Then he took the cup and blessed it, and gave it to them, saying:

Jesus: Trinket alle daraus; das ist mein Blut des neuen Testaments, welches vergossen wird für viele zur Vergebung der Sünden. Ich sage euch: Ich werde von nun an nicht mehr von diesem Gewächs des Weinstocks trinken bis an den Tag da ich's neu trinken werde mit euch in meines Vaters Reich.

Jesus: Drink you all of this; this is my blood of the new testament which will be shed for many for the remission of sins. I say unto you, from now on I shall drink no more of the fruit of the vine until that day when I drink it again with you where my Father reigns high above.

Jesus's prophecy of his betrayal comes at 0:06, and, as the reader will by now expect, the word *verraten* (betray) itself is marked by the interval of a tritone (0:15); further, at 0:28 the word *wehe* (woe) is described with the devil's chord. Judas makes his inquiry at 0:53, and Jesus's simple confirmation is heard at 1:02. The action shifts from Judas to the Eucharist; Jesus blesses first the bread (1:29) and then in much more leisurely terms the wine (1:53).

Mirroring the pair of alto numbers, we now have a pair of soprano pieces, first an arioso, then an aria. Both are accompanied by two oboes d'amore and continuo. The soprano line is marked with a 1 by Bach, indicating perhaps that the forces here are drawn from the daughters of Zion. This is followed by another recitative featuring Jesus, who talks of the impending scattering of the sheep—another reference to prophecy—described in emphatic sixteenth-note chords in the string accompaniment.

The first of a number of iterations of one of the best-known chorales—"Erkenne mich, mein Hüter" (Remember Me, My Savior)—follows (no. 15). The chorale was well known to and clearly much loved by Bach and his congregation. It is known even today—and was popularized at the famous concert in Central Park by Simon and Garfunkel, who sang of being mistaken, confused, forsaken, and misused, notes of self-regard and self-pity that Bach and his peers would not have found particularly endearing.

The chorale returns a number of times, with different texts: a half-step lower as no. 17, "Ich will hier bei dir stehen" (I Will Stand Here by Thee), with the same harmonization, and again in Part 2, no. 44, "Befiel du deine Wege" (Entrust Your Ways to Him), a half-step lower, in D major, in a different harmonization. It reappears in no. 54 to the best-known text, "O Haupt voll Blut und Wunden" (O Head Full of Blood and Wounds), different yet again, and a fifth and last time as no. 62, "Wenn ich einmal soll scheiden" (When I at Last Shall Part), in A minor, in a highly intricate chromatic harmonization. The first five statements have ended in the major key. Not so this last time.

In the following recitative, no. 16, the focus turns to the drama of Peter, when he famously remarks that no matter what others might do, he for one will never desert his Lord. Jesus's reply is well known: Before the cock crows in the morning, Peter will have denied him not once, but three times—a suggestion that Peter refutes firmly. Listen for the melismatic portrayal of the rooster, in Jesus's words. As one might expect, the four notes of the rooster's cry form the augmented sixth, or devil's chord (echoed by the Evangelist much later, when in no. 38 the much-delayed third denial and shocked recoil of Peter occur). Another statement of the passion chorale, first heard as no. 15, follows immediately, and the words this time play a significant dramatic role, ironically echoing the promise just made in the previous recitative by Peter: "Ich will hier bei dir stehen" (I will stand by you).

The duty of standing by Jesus takes specific form in the recitative (no. 18) in which Jesus, in the Garden of Gethsemane, expresses the troubled state of his soul, commented upon in the next number by a tenor soloist in arioso, punctuated by the chorus, who sing a chorale. The orchestration for this arioso is full and quite complex. One striking feature is a continuous pulsing figure in the continuo line, of groups of repeated sixteenth-notes. It is followed by a tenor aria, also with choral interpolations, which has an oboe solo obbligato and is one of the more well-known numbers in the work. It leads into the recitative (no. 19) in which Jesus prays that, if possible, the cup of suffering will pass from him: "Doch nicht wie ich will, sondern wie du willt" (Nevertheless not as I will, but as you will). Another paired arioso–aria group follows, this time for bass, the latter dwelling on the word *gerne*—"gladly" will I drink the cup without complaining, as the Savior did. Besides a statement of solidarity, the cup idea clearly takes us back to the Eucharist instituted earlier. This da capo aria is in G minor and in triple time.

Numbers 19, 21, 24, and 26 depict the action in the garden; the disciples cannot stay awake with him, and as he prays a great crowd arrives, led by Judas and including the chief priests and the elders of the people. Judas kisses Jesus and departs; Jesus is seized.

Then follows a remarkable linked pair of numbers. Number 27 is for a pair of soloists, soprano and alto, powerless as their Lord is taken, punctuated with three choral outbursts, homophonic: "Lasst ihn, haltet, bindet nicht!" (Leave him, stop it, bind him not), which leads directly into a long and furious G minor fugue, in triple time, for double chorus, with a running sixteenth-note subject, calling down thunder and lightning on the tormentors. Meanwhile, there is brief resistance, as one of the disciples draws his sword and cuts off the ear of the high priest's servant, before the disciples scatter and are left alone.

Part 1 ends with a large chorus, a setting of the chorale "O Mensch, bewein' dein Sünde groß" (O Man, Bewail Your Dreadful Sins). The orchestration is rich, busy, and complex; the two choirs are united, with three polyphonic underparts and the cantus firmus chorale in the soprano line. The chorus originally was included in the 1723 version of the *St. John Passion*. There is also a well-known choral prelude in the *Orgelbüchlein* (BWV 622). This concluding movement of Part 1 is more than six minutes long, as long as the last chorus of the whole work.

As we move into the even more intense Part 2, let us first pause for a while and contemplate in the mind's eye the title page of the autograph manuscript—the score earlier described, over which Bach took such trouble. On the lower right there is an irregular circular stain, about nine centimeters in diameter. It might be entertaining to examine this close up. It has all the appearance of having been made by a wineglass. Let's hope so.

The key of the concluding number of Part 1 was the reassuring E major. The opening number of Part 2, no. 30, is similarly ambitious in scale, but now we are in B minor, a key always colored with spiritual intensity in Bach. This aria is an alto solo drawn from choir 1, the choir of the daughters of Zion (if Bach is indeed following Picander's intentions) with chorus interpolations from choir 2, the chorus of the faithful, a series of stately fugal comments, The number is in triple time, and the careful listener will hear frequent hemiolas. The number is scored for two orchestras, the first of which has a flute and oboe d'amore doubling the top line. This device gives an astringent flavor to the sound. The chorus entries are accompanied by the second orchestra, which is strings only, and the emotional temperature is lower. We do not think often enough about Bach the orchestrator; though he did not have the resources of, shall we say, Sibelius or Berlioz, he was highly resourceful and plotted orchestral effects carefully.

The following recitative (no. 31) takes Jesus before Caiaphas. Listen for the augmented sixth chord on the words "auf dass sie ihn töteten" (that he might be put to death), spelled by the tones E-flat–C–A–F-sharp; by now this harmony will be very recognizable. A slacking of the emotional pitch comes with a chorale, before, in no. 33, we take up the narrative once more; in this recitative, two "falsche Zeugen" (false witnesses), in a brief fugal arietta, testify they heard Jesus threaten to pull down the temple and rebuild it in three days. Recitative/arioso no. 34, for tenor, is accompanied by thirty-nine staccato strokes, for two oboes marked by Bach, unusually, with staccato marks; with viola da gamba chords of three or four notes, also to be played detached; and by the continuo. It describes the scourging of Jesus and his silent endurance of it, some commentators think, and we get a glimpse of Bach the numerologist at work. Thirty-nine strokes, in ten measures; Psalm 39, verse 10 (King James version), reads, "Remove thy stroke away from me: I am consumed by the blow of thine hand." There are a number of books about Bach's slightly occult symbolism, some of them a touch nutty. But there is no doubt that Bach was himself quite preoccupied with such symbolism. He did, after all, work the notes B (= B-flat)–A–C–H (= B-natural) into his music on a number of occasions, for example at the end of the last *contrapunctus* in his *Art of the Fugue.* Ruth Tatlow's *Riddle of the Number Alphabet* (1991) is one of the more plausible studies and is worth a look. Surprisingly, no one has yet written a whodunit of *The Da Vinci Code* type based on the life of Bach. Then again perhaps someone has, or will now take up this hint.

The gamba, already to the fore, now has one of the great solos of the repertoire—the lower line of a tricky tenor aria, "Geduld!" (Be Patient!). The tenor soloist and gamba occupy almost the same tessitura and often overlap. The only other accompanying instrument is the organ. Jesus has in fact been patient for some time, not responding to taunts and questions. This situation now changes, in no. 36, and we hear two choral interpolations, both for double choir, between which Jesus is pushed around and beaten by the crowd. The virtuosity of the chorus is once again called forth in no. 37, a chorale that follows straight on from the uproar of nos. 36B and 36D, the two choruses.

The drama of Peter comes to its climax in no. 38, which is the recitative in which the third denial of Peter and his self-appalled reaction occur. It is interesting to compare the parallel moment in the *St. John Passion*; both portray the weeping of Peter in long, chromatic melismata. This passion treats the moment with relatively less complexity than the earlier *St. John Passion.* Listen also for the Evangelist's echo of Jesus's earlier representation of the cock. Three of the four notes are the same, but the harmony is cooler—a regular dominant seventh, instead of the augmented sixth.

Aria (alto), "Erbarme dich" (Have Mercy), with violin obbligato (CD Track 15)

Erbarme dich, mein Gott,	Have mercy, my God,
um meiner Zähren willen!	for the sake of my tears!
Schaue hier, Herz und Auge	See here, heart and eyes
weint vor dir bitterlich.	Weep bitterly before you.
Erbarme dich, mein Gott.	Have mercy, my God.

The lamenting and the call for mercy are Peter's, whose weeping after the third cock crow has just been depicted. The aria is for alto soloist, in the key of B minor, often chosen by Bach as the key of lament, and of course the key of the Great Mass. The rhythm is that of the siciliano, comparing thus with the opening chorus of the *Passion*. The violin obbligato calls for a high measure of art, and the texture is quite exposed both for the vocal soloist and the violinist; Bach specifies that the continuo line will be played pizzicato throughout, and the vocal line is extremely high, going up to high E on seven separate occasions. Bach Collegium Japan use the brilliant British countertenor Robin Blaze on this recording. All great altos measure themselves by how well they can perform this aria; Christa Ludwig, David Daniels, Alfred Deller, Kathleen Ferrier, and Yoshikazu Mera (Mera is well known to admirers of Bach Collegium Japan) have all recorded it.

Long, decorated phrases for both violin and alto soloists characterize the piece. There is a long violin introduction, over the pulsing pizzicato bass, and the alto begins with a phrase right at the top of the range (0:54). The writing is very chromatic throughout (for example, at 1:13ff) and includes much material drawn from the augmented sixth (devil's) chord (1:22, 1:28, 1:53, 4:53, and elsewhere). One of the most beautiful and taxing passages comes at 2:16 on the word *Zähren* (tears), a slow-rising passage, going from middle C-sharp to high D and giving the singer nowhere plausible to breathe for well over ten seconds. This phrase brings the first section of the aria to rest, in the dominant key of F-sharp minor, and leads to new material at 2:54 with long, drawn-out notes at the start of three successive measures. Vocally, the climax of the work comes with a high melismatic passage over three measures (4:58–5:08), and a violin postlude brings us to the end.

A chorale follows (no. 40), the theme of which is the possibility of returning to Jesus after a transgression.

The focus now turns from the drama of Peter, henceforth the rock on which the Church is built (Greek *petros* = rock), to Judas's repentance and suicide; now we realize the momentous words of Jesus from the earlier Last Supper recitative, when he said it would be better for the man who betrays his Lord if he had never been born. In Buddhist terms, he was referring to the working out of karma, rather than being driven by a vengeful spirit.

In the following recitative, the high priests plan the death of Jesus (to be accomplished by their conferring the responsibility on Pontius Pilate). On the word *töteten* (put to death), for Bach decorates the continuo line with the notes A–F-sharp–D-sharp–B-sharp—the augmented sixth once again. Judas, repenting of what he has done, attempts to return the thirty silver pieces to the high priests. In a double chorus they decline the money, and in a continuation of the recitative Judas casts the money down and, to the accompaniment of yet another devil's chord, hangs himself. The high priests, in a brief duet, decide that the blood money cannot go in the temple coffers. This side drama is resolved in recitative no. 43, when the money is used to buy a piece of land, the celebrated Potters' Field, to be used for the burial of strangers—which is, to this day, what we call the largest publicly funded cemetery in the world, the paupers' burial ground on Hart's Island in New York City. Before this drama, however, in no. 42, a bass aria (drawn from choir 2, the assembly of the faithful), a resolute soul comments on the return of the blood money. This aria, in G major and accompanied by ripieno strings with a solo violin obbligato, is as stalwart a piece as Bach ever wrote. The singer begs to have Jesus back; the logic of the claim is that Judas has repented and cast aside the money. But it is not to be.

We now shift from Peter and Judas to a third and enormously powerful drama—that of Pontius Pilate, the Roman governor, whom the

High Priests are hoping to maneuver into solving for them the dilemma presented by Jesus. This part of the story is well known—the acceptance by Jesus of the title King of the Jews when questioned by Pilate (a political challenge), his refusal to answer the high priests and elders (a doctrinal evasion), and his final silence, which "astonishes Pilate mightily." We turn to the gesture of holiday-time amnesty; Pilate offers to release one individual at this holiday time (hoping the crowd will choose Jesus). In a resounding augmented-sixth chord, pitched high in the vocal ranges, the crowd cry for the release of the notorious criminal Barabbas, and in passages built around the same harmonies, in the form of a furious fugue, call for the crucifixion of Jesus.

What evil has he done, inquires Pilate (no. 47). Comes the faithful's reply in a soprano recitative-arioso (no. 48): Nothing, except to give to the blind their sight, to lepers their legs, comfort to those who mourn, and the word of God to all. This arioso, accompanied by continuo and two oboes da caccia, is marked by Bach *a battuta*, in strict time, like the ticking of a clock. (Another number in the *St. Matthew Passion* so marked is no. 56, the arioso associated with Simon of Cyrene.) The oboe lines move in parallel thirds throughout, and they are retained thus for the soprano aria that follows, "Aus Liebe will mein Heiland sterben" (For Love Will My Savior Die), The oboes are joined by a flute. But there is no continuo, no bass line, and we are as far from the earthly as it is possible to go, before the crowd cry out yet again (in no. 50).

Pilate washes his hands (literally and figuratively) and refuses responsibility: "Ich bin unschuldig an dem Blut dieses Gerechten, sehet ihr zu" (I am innocent of the blood of this righteous man; you see to it). The crowd willingly take on the blood guilt, on behalf of themselves and their children. He releases Barabbas and gives Jesus over to be scourged and crucified.

An alto soloist comments in an arioso/aria pair of numbers, before the soldiers mock Jesus as King of the Jews and place the crown of thorns on his head, leading to the apotheosis of the Passion Chorale, heard several times already but now associated with the crown: "O Haupt voll Blut und Wunden" (O Sacred Head, Sore Wounded), the text by which it is best known today. We await one further iteration in no. 62, when the choir comment on the death of Jesus and contemplate their own mortality.

Besides the crucifixion, two further human dramas await us. First, Simon of Cyrene, an outsider, is forced to carry the cross. This is the moment also to recall the great solo cantata *Ich will den Kreuzstab gerne tragen* (I Will Gladly Carry the Cross) (BWV 56).

Evoking Simon and his task, while gladly taking up the cross, the bass soloist has an arioso (no. 56), accompanied by sustained chords on the viola da gamba, while two flutes provide decoration with groups of three paired notes, in parallel sixths and thirds. This is marked *a battuta*, in strict time, as was no. 48. The following aria, also for the bass, is another high point of the gamba solo repertoire. It is tricky, complex, and over six minutes long, and it tests the bass soloist as well the violist. The aura of faith and peace prepared by this aria is soon shattered by the crowd in the long recitative with choral interruptions, no. 58, the latter of which, no. 58D, ends with the chorus in unison, spitefully reminding anyone who will listen that Christ claimed to be God's son. It is once again the oboe da caccias' chance, in a paired arioso/aria for alto. The recitative "Ach Golgatha," with long phrases, is especially demanding for the oboists, and most thoughtful conductors will take the ubiquitous fermata at the end of the arioso literally and give the poor soloists a break, because what comes next is tougher still for the continuo players. We move on from Golgotha to a playful aria for alto (from choir 1, therefore a daughter of Zion) with paired obbligato oboes da caccia—playful because salvation is now at hand. The soloist seems to recall the opening chorus of the whole work, depicting Christ's outstretched arms and the word "Come," to which chorus 2 (the chorus of the faithful) ask repeatedly, "Wohin?" (Where?). In another shift for the chorus comes the mockery of Jesus in recitative 61A, when he calls in Hebrew for the God (the Father) who has forsaken the Son, and after the death of Jesus in no. 61E both choruses now have to shift yet again for the final statement of the Passion Chorale (no. 62). The harmonization of this last chorale is worth studying. Those who wish to examine Bach's chorale harmonizations in depth should look at the one-volume compilation by Schmieder. In an earlier time, composition students might have been required to take down the chorale line from dictation (i.e., by listening to it and writing it down). They might then have been instructed to harmonize it in the style of Bach, after which they would have had to take down Bach's version, also from dictation, an experience sufficiently humbling to dissuade many (including the present writer) from pursuing composition as a career. The chorales may also be seen as BWV 250 to BWV 438.

Following the death of Jesus, the recitative continuo team have to portray the furious upheavals—the rending of the temple veil, the earthquakes, the disgorging of the dead from their graves. There are scales and tremulations, in thirty-second-notes, while the poor Evangelist, after two and a half hours of hard work, is taken four times up to B-flat, just a step below treble C. Next comes what must be, dramatically speaking, the most audacious moment of all—when the Roman centurions are told that this was truly the Son of God. Numerologists have found in this chorus Bach's signature: B (letter 2) + A (1) + C (3) + H (8) = 14, the number of notes in the piece.

The final aria for bass (no. 65, "Mache dich, mein Herze, rein") may open with an excursus on tempo. This aria certainly reflects Joseph of Arimathea's personal feelings about burying Jesus, though many feel the aria embodies a Christian's acceptance of redemption. Here Bach reserves perhaps the most audacious musical decision for last, as he gives bass an aria in 12/8 time, which would be a siciliano were it not much more obviously a gigue. I believe that we can know it to be a gigue for three solid reasons. The obbligato instruments have long phrases with relatively few opportunities to breathe, and at any tempo much less than dotted quarter-note = 60 it would be unplayable; the bass solo line imposes similar constraints. Most persuasive, however, are the phrasing marks in the autograph score. It is most unusual for Bach to mark up his music in this way, and when he does so there is always a story behind it. Recitative no. 34 in the *St. Matthew Passion* is a case in point, as we have already seen. Lovers of *The Well-Tempered Clavier* may remember Book 2, no. 22, the fugue in B-flat minor, which starts with the notes B-flat–C–D-flat. Ordinarily, we would follow the default rule: If it is stepwise, legato; if skipwise, detach. Bach marked these three notes with sharp dashes—not just dots. At the end of the fugue we see why; there comes a moment when two voices in parallel thirds have the subject going upward, while two other voices have it in thirds but inverted. The effect is a startling pair of staccato chords. The whole of no. 65 is full of phrasing marks—rows of sixteenths marked as slurred pairs, and most strikingly, the first four notes of the oboe parts are two pairs of slurred quarter- and half-note units. To lovers of the keyboard suites and partitas (throughout both sets, but note especially the gigues at the end of the G Minor English Suite and the G Major French Suite, and the B-flat Major Partita), and the sprightly fugues in *The Well-Tempered Clavier* (especially Book 2, C-sharp minor, E minor, F major, to specify three), this means jigs. The reason is that the Italian giga, which Bach especially loved, was traditionally played on a instrument called that—a giga, which the Irish would call a kit—a tiny traveler's violin, with a bow so short that in compound triple time the phrasing had to be two notes on the down bow, one on the up. And this is how we must also phrase the gigues in the keyboard music. The French gigue is more sober, and even in the so-called French Suites, Bach is writing gigas. Listen to Couperin's gigues, up against Bach's, and you will hear the difference. Even the great Jig Fugue in G Major for organ, BWV 577, is a boozy affair. The French are a lot more serious.

So the tempo of the bass aria is a little problematic. The *St. Matthew Passion* volume of the *Bach Neue-Ausgabe* complete edition of Bach's works that I am lucky enough to be able to work from was used by its first owner, Peter Gram Swing, who founded the Swarthmore College Music Department and taught at Tanglewood for over twenty-five years. Swing was also a co-conspirator of P. D. Q. Bach (Peter Schickele) in a jolly jeu d'esprit called *Liebeslieder Polkas* (still available as a CD). Swing used the *St. Matthew Passion* as a conductor's copy. He marked chorus no. 1 (a siciliano) at sixty-four beat pulses per minute, and no. 65 at forty-eight beats per minute. The mystery is compounded by some emphatic pencil annotations in Swing's vocal score (the short score he seems to have used as a rehearsal copy with the chorus at Swarthmore): "A gigue—This has some joy—a dance—Joy." I greatly regret never having met Peter Swing, whose music library came to us at the Putney School after his death and whose life was so clearly full of love, energy, and wisdom. But most of all, I would have greatly enjoyed asking him what he could have meant by that metronome marking!

Bach Collegium Japan take Simon's aria at fifty-six to the minute—
and it seems a little slow. Frans Brüggen starts at fifty-nine—and that
seems a little fast, as he found also, for he settled down to fifty-seven—
just about right. John Eliot Gardiner likes fifty-three, and Solti in 1988
favored the astonishingly slow fifty. Otto Klemperer in 1962 thought
thirty-four to the minute was about right, which would make Peter
Swing's forty-eight sound quite jaunty by comparison. On the whole,
I was thinking, *I don't know about forty-eight*. Then I came across Karl
Richter's recording of 1952, and he chose the entirely convincing tempo
of forty-eight to the minute. So there we are, Peter Swing, maybe you
win. The reviewer in the local newspaper *News of Delaware County*,
writing on April 12, 1979, certainly thought so, reporting that "Mark
Shibuya . . . delivered the aria with moving sincerity."

The drama is almost done, but first the chorus has one more burst
of cynicism (in no. 66B), when they represent the high priests and the
Pharisees, urging Pilate to set a guard on the tomb so that the disciples
will be unable to stage a resurrection. Pilate's last act is to let them
know (in 66C) that if they need watchmen, they can be provided.

Number 67 portrays the burial of Jesus with four accompanied
arioso phrases, for bass, tenor, alto, and soprano in turn, punctuated
by tender chordal commentary from the chorus. This predominantly
homophonic style persists through the last chorus of BWV 244, the *St.
Matthew Passion*, in triple time, and in C minor, as was the last number
in BWV 245, the *St. John Passion*.

Mass in B Minor

For many, Bach's Mass in B Minor (BWV 232) is the high point not just of Bach's music, but of all music. It is such a massive work (about two hours long) and in some ways oddly remote from us. The text is in Latin, for one thing, not the vernacular language (German) that Bach, along with Martin Luther, so clearly loved. It has none of the familiar mixture of aria, recitative, and chorus that we know from the cantatas and the passions; nor does it have the alternation of biblical narrative with reflection and commentary that we have come to find so familiar in these works. These factors are what give the atmosphere of humanity to the passions. With the Mass we seem to be on a different plane. It feels somehow like Bach's testament. And yet it is worth remarking that when he came to write his testament, it seems to have been in the form of a simple chorale harmonization, which legend has it the blind Bach dictated on his deathbed to his son-in-law Altnikol:

Vor deinen Thron tret ich hiermit	Before your throne I now appear,
O Gott, und dich demütig bitt	O God, and humble beg you
Wend dein genädig Angesicht	Not to turn your gracious face
Von mir, dem armen Sünder nicht.	From me, a sinner.

The legend is a legend, it must be said. Wolff, in an essay called "The Deathbed Chorale: Exposing a Myth" in *Bach: Essays on His Life and Music* (1991, 282–94), shows that Bach was occupied with revising an earlier composition in his last days. He did have the help of an amanuensis, but dreamy scenes of the old boy tearfully calling out the names of notes to the faithful Altnikol while others of his family assumed pious postures and wept, in the style of a mannerist painterly fantasy, seem to be just that—dreams. This chorale (BWV 668) is now usually published at the end of *The Art of the Fugue*, following the so-called unfinished last fugue, which, Wolff demonstrates in another essay in the same volume, was not unfinished at all.

Many mysteries surround the Mass. It is perhaps odd that Bach should set a Latin text; it is strange that a work presented as a whole should, so far as we know, never have been performed in its entirety. Odd, too, is the compositional history. It was not assembled in its present form until just before his death; an early version was a Missa (consisting of the present Kyrie and Gloria) presented in 1733 to Augustus II, elector of Saxony, as part of a plan to woo him into appointing Bach as court composer. The Credo, the heart of the work, may not have been written (or perhaps a better term would be *assembled*) until the 1740s, though some scholars believe it existed in fundamentally its present form as early as 1732, and we know that some sections were composed much earlier. The Crucifixus, for example, first saw light as the second movement of BWV 12, a cantata dating from 1714 (Weimar). Whatever the chronology, it is known that the Credo was presented to Augustus as part of the Missa, but it is not known whether it was performed at that time—though the Kyrie and Gloria were heard then. Perhaps the Credo was heard also, but we simply do not know; there is no evidence that the Credo was performed until 1786, thirty-six years after the composer's death, when it was conducted by his son C. P. E. Bach. The Sanctus, by contrast, existed in preliminary form as early as 1724. So far as we know, the Mass as a whole was not performed until 1859. Questions heavily outnumber answers. There is an academic heavy industry devoted to the explication of the Mass in B Minor, as typified by a three-day conference in Belfast in 2007 that ended with a keynote address by Christoph Wolff, "Past, Present, and Future—Perspectives on Bach's B-Minor Mass." The general listener, meantime, has plenty to do of his or her own, in getting to know this wonderful work. That it was, in Bach's mind, one work is perhaps indicated by his writing his usual closing statement "SDG" (Soli Deo gloria—"to the glory of God alone") only at the end of the Dona Nobis Pacem.

Mass in B Minor: A listener's guide

Readers may wish to acquire a recording of the complete Mass. How to choose? These days, we can sample music and find many CD reviews on the Internet. Remember that practitioners of Bach usually have recorded most or all of the choral music, and as you listen you will begin to favor certain approaches. Some of us have several recordings (the present writer confessing to as many as five).

The whole work consists of twenty-seven sections. It is a great deal to take in all at once. Setting one's computer or CD player to repeat one or a few sections (not necessarily consecutive) is a good idea. Having the Mass on the CD player in one's car and just absorbing it is a very good plan. Those who like to look at the score have plenty of choices. Christoph Wolff recently published a facsimile of Bach's autograph manuscript, beautifully produced. It is rather expensive, but many college and university libraries will have it. The Bach Gesellschaft edition can be downloaded free as a PDF file. Study scores and vocal "reductions" (in which the orchestral parts are arranged as a piano accompaniment) are easy to come by. Some readers will be lucky enough to find a community chorus or the like rehearsing the B Minor Mass for performance. There is no better way to get to know this wonderful music. The chorus will have to have plenty of sopranos, however, for the choral writing is often for five rather than four voices, the sopranos being divided into two sections.

I. Kyrie

The Kyrie movement, in three sections, sets the Greek prayer "Kyrie eleison, Christe eleison, Kyrie eleison" (Lord have mercy, Christ have mercy, Lord have mercy). The first Kyrie eleison begins by announcing the home key of B minor in a slow, solid, huge chordal homophonic statement, from the midst of which two three-note snatches of soprano melody drift off. Listen for the cadence at the end of the section, when the bass steps down from the home note by a whole-step, then another, and then a half-step, to land on the root note of F-sharp major, the dominant note of the scale of B minor. This is a cadential idiom that

Bach repeatedly met in his early Vivaldi studies. This type of cadence always presages something with more movement and a steady rhythmic texture, which is precisely what we get here. We set off into a long fugue, in four-time, the pulse of which seems to want to be about twice the pace of the opening largo. There is a lengthy orchestral introduction, in which two flutes, doubled by two oboes d'amore, announce the subject—and what a subject it is. It has a number of repeated notes, as if Bach were seeking to be rather definite about the tonality, but within one measure we have some rather tense chromatic colors—intrusive sharps and flats that push against the tonality. Two other feature of this subject should be noted, for they come back again and again in this section. First are the two pairs of notes, a semitone apart, sliding downward; these are sometimes known as *sospiri*, or "sighs." Bach uses this idiom frequently to generate the sense of a high emotional temperature, even on occasion to depict tears. As the movement goes on, you will hear Bach chain together large numbers of these sospiri. The second feature is an unusually wide leap in the melody, of a seventh, following what feels like a further doubling of the pace, in a winding run of sixteenth-notes.

The fugue winds along for some time and comes to an intermediate rest when the voices make a cadence in F-sharp minor, the dominant key, the first of several modulations or key changes that Bach makes. Listen for the arrival in a major key at one point. Listen also for several *pedal points*, where the basses come to rest and hold on to a note while the other voices waft kaleidoscopically above—a pedal point in Bach often foretells a cadence.

The first Kyrie is long, and very intense, and when the Christe eleison comes, we are ready for a change. The change is multifaceted. First, we have a major key, that of D major. Bach's selection of B minor for the whole has been in part a preparation for the arrival of D major, the key of trumpets and drums, the key of glory (as we shall shortly hear), of the resurrection, and ultimately of the establishment of eternal peace, as we hear in the very last movement of the work the "Dona nobis pacem" (Give us peace). For now, however, we have a duet for two sopranos with obbligato violins, not solo, but tutti (played in unison). The sopranos sometimes glide to and fro together, in harmonizing thirds or sixths (note that sixths and thirds are inversions of each other; D upward to F-sharp is a third, counting top and bottom notes, while F-sharp upward to D is a sixth).

The question Bach had to face was what to do with the second Kyrie. It would have been clumsy to turn the whole movement into a da capo aria. I will leave readers to make their own characterizations of the section. Suffice it to say that it is a fugue, and while perhaps it does not have the drama of the opening Kyrie, it is quite intense harmonically, and the chromatic opening of the subject contrasts strikingly with that of the first Kyrie.

II. Gloria

It would seem like material for the musicologists, were it not for Bach himself obviously important, that the Gloria ("Gloria in excelsis Deo, et in terra pax hominibus bonae voluntatis"—Glory be to God in the highest, and on Earth peace to men of goodwill) has a symmetrical structure. It has nine movements: chorus, chorus, solo (soprano); chorus, duet (soprano, tenor), chorus; solo, solo, chorus. The number three represents the Trinity, a fundamental doctrine of the Christian creed. The section "Domine Deus" (Lord God), is at the center of the Gloria, and it is likely not coincidental that this text, which refers to Jesus as the only begotten Son of God, is a duet, for low and high voices. When we come to the Credo, we will find a similar nine-part structure, this time with the Crucifixus at the center.

Gloria and Et in terra pax (CD Tracks 16 and 17)

Gloria in excelsis Deo,	Glory be to God in the highest,
Et in terra pax hominibus bonae voluntatis.	And on earth peace to men of goodwill.

The chorus is for soprano 1 and 2, alto, tenor, and bass. The orchestration is for two flutes, two oboes, three trumpets, timpani, first and second violins, violas, cellos, continuo (cello, bass, bassoon, organ).

We open with a short sinfonia, appropriately in triple time (written in eighth- and sixteenth-notes, Bach's clear stipulation that the pace should be quite brisk), and in the glorious key of D major, the key of trumpets. Bach is writing for D trumpets; these are transposing instruments, which means that a written C sounds as a D. Bach's trumpeters would have an assortment of crooks and an extra bit of tubing, to permit easy playing in a variety of keys.

In the first nine seconds, continuo and timpani, supported by the brass and wind instruments, insist upon D major, straying only to the dominant of the home chord (A). The two timpani are in any case tuned to D and A, so subtlety is not the object of the exercise here; affirmation is. The continuo holds the triple pulse, as do the trumpets, while everyone else (flutes, oboes, upper strings) chatters in a series of sixteenth-note arpeggio figures. *Arpeggios* (from the Italian for "harp") are scattered, or broken, chords. Their purpose here is to emphasize the underlying chordal nature of the first measures. Within a short time, Bach lands on the dominant (A) chord and stays there for three measures (0:07–0:10). Once he brings this stasis to an end, it is in favor of harmonic movement. For a few seconds the drums back off, while the trumpets supply the staccato pulses, one per measure, for the most part. The woodwinds and upper strings continue with the sixteenth-note phrases, but now the writing is more stepwise than skipwise (melodic rather than arpeggiated). The big difference is in the continuo, which begins to march also stepwise in a series of downward sweeps that take us first briefly (0:12) to the somewhat remote key of E minor (the subdominant of the implied B minor), and then by repeating the sequence one note lower back home (0:18) to D, the trumpets decorating this all the while with little jabs and flourishes. Now it is the continuo's time to strut some arpeggios (0:18–0:23), before everyone comes to the D major home cadence, with trumpet trills and a drum tattoo of four sixteenth-notes, and the chorus enters (0:25).

The vocal entries are staggered: altos first, then two measures later the tenors, with identical material, and then first and second sopranos and basses. The whole series of entries lasts a bare nine seconds (0:25–0:33), but how thrilling it is. The first syllable of "Gloria," with its wonderful open vowel, gets two full measures in each of the two leading voices. The orchestra returns with the downward-striding continuo material we have heard already, but in a different key this time, and when they come "home" it is to the dominant key of A, not the tonic key of D (0:41), and it is in the key of A that the chorus now enters, led this time by the first sopranos, followed at the same distance of two measures by the second sopranos, then two measures later by the other voices, singing homophonically (i.e., in chords). However, they are not this time displaced by the orchestra, pressing on instead with new material. We have already had the words "in excelsis," but now the second syllable is stretched over seven beats (more than two measures), then followed by a sixteenth-note decorative figure, first by both soprano groups, singing in thirds, then by tenors and altos, singing in sixths (0:50–0:56). The basses do not get this figure; their duty is to strut, with the continuo, in another arpeggio progression, for a full six measures before making landfall with another cadence, firmly in the dominant key of A major. Of course, there is no drum tattoo on the pickup to this cadence, as there was earlier, for the dominant (fifth) note of the dominant is E, and the drums are tuned to D and A. The timpanist must be content with three hearty whacks when the key of A is reached (1:04, 1:06, 1:08), the third of which introduces the third set of chorus entries, this time with wholly new material, this time fully fugal, and now the first syllable of "gloria" gets almost four full measures in each part. Tenors are followed by altos, basses, first sopranos, and second sopranos, all at a distance of two measures (1:08–1:19), but shortly the polyphonic gives way to three measures in which the chorus moves in decisive harmonic unity from the home key of D to its dominant, once again (1:20–1:23).

That blaze of voices, trumpets, and drums is it, so far as the musical and thematic development is concerned. We have a return to the "excelsis" material, with voices in paired sixths and thirds, leading to a final home cadence. This last time, though, the timpanist gets four sixteenth-notes, to lead us in a segue, without a break, into the "et in terra pax." And the trumpets get a break. They will not be heard from again until later in the "et in terra pax," where they do, however, get the decisive last word in the form of the final fugal entry.

"Et in terra pax" is almost three times as long as its predecessor, and it is in common time (4/4) rather than triple time. The pulses of the two are connected, however; the eighth-note is about the same length in both sections. Appropriately, the voices enter together, in harmony, and immediately take us off toward the flat side of the key system by going into G, the subdominant of D major. Until now, the progression has been always in the opposite direction, toward the sharp side and the dominant of A major. Now we have a slackening of tension. This air of peace is sustained with the aid of several pedal points in the continuo, which sits first on the note G for three measures, then on B for three measures, then (after the chorus becomes silent) on a low E, for an astonishing four whole measures, this last pedal point being marked "t.s." for *tasto solo*, meaning to be played without the accompanying harmony, while the instruments drift in sospiri, in antiphonal choirs of woodwind and strings. The continuo line picks up the sospiri idea, descending in two measures of slurred stepwise sospiri, before this remarkable moment of peace gives way to a protracted fugue, led off by the first sopranos. The fugue subject is based on the same material as earlier. But now there is a long and florid countersubject in sixteenth-notes that each voice has in turn. First sopranos are followed by altos, tenors, basses, and finally by the second sopranos. The movement settles down after a while, and there is some lovely antiphonal writing, with back-and-forth between singers and orchestra, before the climax of the movement, which is marked by the arrival on the scene of the trumpets, and their friend the timpanist, to whom Bach gives a healthy-sounding drumroll (3:28). The high point is human, however, in the bass line (3:49–4:00) when the basses intone, in three solid long notes, the word "pax," three times. This is clearly a prayer, or a blessing, and it is answered (4:00–4:16) by a threefold invocation of peace from the chorus. So now we think back to the three pedal points just referred to. Nothing is accidental in Bach.

Gloria, continued

The Laudamus Te (We praise you, O God) is essentially a duet, between violin obbligato and soprano solos, with decorative accompaniment from continuo and the upper strings. The long obbligato introduction (forty-five seconds out of a four-minute aria) sounds as if it might be from a lost concerto or sonata, though we do not have direct evidence of this. It is as if Bach were making a calculation about his audience's capacity for patient attention, for the movement that follows, Gratias agimus tibi (We give thanks to You), is a rather foursquare fugue, which first saw the light as the opening chorus of Cantata BWV 29 of 1731 (one of Bach's election cantatas). The words of the original, "Wir danken dir, Gott" (We thank Thee, O God), are a German translation of Gratias agimus tibi. The key is D major, and the trumpets and drums make quite a foil for what follows next.

The fifth section, at the dead center of Bach's plan for the Gloria, is a duet for tenor and soprano, with a flute obbligato. Importantly, it is in G major, the subdominant of the D major, which it follows. This shift toward the flat side of the tonal circle, G, has one fewer sharp than D. A similar shift occurs in the Credo, when the "Et in unum" sets off in G major after the D major fanfare brilliance of the ending of the movement that precedes it. The text, "Domine Deus," speaks of the lord God as the Lamb, and the only Son of God. The words seems to rotate—lamb of God, son of God—back and forth, as if Bach would have us ponder the mystery of a god who would permit the sacrifice of his own son.

The "Qui tollis" (Who takes away the sins of the world) returns us to B minor and feels as though it could be a crucifixion chorus from a passion. It is in fact related to cantata BWV 46 from 1723, which fell on a Passion Week, there a revision of part of the opening chorus of Cantata no. 46 (1723), "Schauet doch und sehet" (Behold and see if there be any sorrow like unto His sorrow). B minor is the key also of the aria Qui sedes (Who sits at the right hand of God), for alto solo with oboe d'amore obbligato.

The notes of suffering implicit in B minor are set aside by the arrival of a hunting horn, accompanied by two jaunty bassoons, in the bass solo "Quoniam tu solus sanctus" (For You only are holy), and the Gloria and Bach's original 1733 project end with the D major polyphonic chorus (for five voices) "Cum Sancto Spiritu" (Who with the holy spirit), a blur of vocal agility, drums, and trumpets.

III. Credo

Like the Gloria, and on a similar scale, the Credo (sometimes known as the Symbolum Nicenum or Nicene Creed) has its own cohesive structure, based also on nine parts. Parts 1 through 3 affirm faith in God the creator and in God the son; parts 4 through 6 deal with the life, suffering, death, and resurrection of the living Christ, with the crucifixion as the middle element in this group; parts 7 through 9 treat of the Holy Spirit, the sacrament of baptism, and the anticipation of resurrection for the believer. There are seven choruses, and only two arias—one a duet for higher voices talking of the incarnation of Christ, the other a priestly bass expounding the doctrine of the Holy Spirit "who proceeds from the Father and the Son, and who with the Father and the Son together is worshipped and glorified."

Here is the scheme, with translation:

> *Credo in unum Deum* (chorus): I believe in one God.
>
> *Patrem omnipotentem* (chorus): I believe in one God, the Father Almighty, maker of heaven and earth, and of all things visible and invisible.
>
> *Et in unum Dominum* (duet, soprano and alto): And in one Lord Jesus Christ, the only begotten Son of God, begotten of the Father before all worlds; God of God, Light of Light, very God of very God; begotten, not made, being of one substance with the Father, by whom all things were made, who, for us men and for our salvation, came down from heaven.
>
> *Et incarnatus est* (chorus): And was incarnate by the Holy Spirit of the Virgin Mary, and was made man.
>
> *Crucifixus* (chorus): And was crucified also for us under Pontius Pilate; He suffered and was buried.
>
> *Et resurrexit* (chorus): And the third day He rose again, according to the Scriptures; and ascended into heaven, and sits on the right hand of the Father; and He shall come again, with glory, to judge the quick and the dead; whose kingdom shall have no end.
>
> *Et in Spiritum Sanctum* (bass solo): And I believe in the Holy Ghost, the Lord and Giver of Life; who proceeds from the Father

and the Son; who with the Father and the Son together is worshipped and glorified; who spoke by the prophets. And I believe in one holy catholic and apostolic Church.

Confiteor (chorus): I acknowledge one baptism for the remission of sins.

Et expecto (chorus): And I look for the resurrection of the dead, and the life of the world to come. Amen.

Credo in unum Deum

This opening chorus is based on the ancient plainchant to which the creed is sung and which we may hear in many churches every Sunday. Here it is woven into a stately fugue, accompanied by the continuo walking along in quarter-notes, eight to a measure. There are two violin lines also, and interestingly, these have independent roles in the fugue. The order of entries is thus tenor, alto, soprano 1, soprano 2, bass, violins 1, violins 2. There is a second set of entries, somewhat similar, but then comes a surprise; shortly before the end of the movement, the basses restate the subject, but this time at half speed. In other words, each note is twice the standard length, and so the subject is stated as a sort of cantus firmus. The theme here is clearly the solidarity, as well as the solidity, of faith.

Patrem omnipotentem

This second chorus is quite different in tenor, with a jaunty subject adapted from the opening movement of BWV 171, a New Year's cantata, perhaps from 1729. The movement is driven as before by the continuo, in eighth-notes now, and still ahead of the chorus in pace. The key is D major (the subdominant of the first movement, and perhaps a more homely or human tonality, and we are not surprised by the entry of one trumpet, joined after a while by its two colleagues, which lead the ensemble out in a blaze of fanfare.

Et in unum Dominum

Bach takes once more a step in the direction of the flat keys. This duet is in G major (the same key as Domine Deus in the Gloria, and for the same reason). The duet "Et in unum Dominum" is set for soprano and alto with two oboes d'amore and strings; really, it is a double duet, similar to that in the fifth movement of BWV 9. Here, the two pairs work material that is approximately canonic, though it is never a canon at the unison. This is definitely a movement that should be listened to repeatedly, and perhaps with the aid of a score. Readers who find canons fascinating should listen to Bach's *Goldberg Variations*, which has a progression of canons at the unison, the second, the third, and then right on to a canon at the octave—and then again a canon at the ninth. In the *Goldbergs*, the answering voice sometimes inverts the first voice's statement. One last recommendation for lovers of canons would be the double canon (four voices) on the Christmas carol "In dulci jubilo" for organ (BWV 608); the carol fits together with itself a distance of one measure (right-hand pinkie and the feet); two other lines, also canonic at the same distance, make up the middle two lines.

Listen in the "Et in unum Dominum" for the contrast between homophonic passages (a third or a sixth apart) and the more polyphonic material.

Et incarnatus est

Back in B minor now, and in triple time, the incarnation of Christ is invoked in a faraway, stately drifting down in quarter-notes of one voice after another (alto, soprano 1, soprano 2, tenor, bass), over a sostenuto pedal point in the continuo, while violins 1 and 2 trade a sixteenth-note figure with more of the slurred pairs of notes we have already identified as sospiri. The slurs are marked as such by Bach, who almost never uses phrasing marks, except where he wishes the phrasing to be unconventional. In this case the slurred notes are across the beat, from weak to strong, which would ordinarily not be slurred, so specific instructions are necessary. Players of the piano will see a similar situation in the B-flat major fugue in the second book of *The Well-Tempered Clavier*. There, too, Bach supplies phrasing to make his unconventional intentions clear. In the present movement there are two wonderful moments, both in the soprano 1 line, where Bach makes use of the hemiola; two measures of triple time become three measures of duple time. What might Bach's symbolic intention be? The text at this point is "ex Maria virgine." Without being overly intricate, this is one of those moments where we must remember that nothing in Bach happens by chance.

Crucifixus

The Crucifixus is based to some extent on the first chorus of a cantata written in 1714 in Weimar. The reworking represents a remarkable improvement on the original, intense yet spare in its focus on the death of Christ. The voices sag downward in a series of sospiri, while the continuo play a chaconne (a repeating passage) of four measures in which the bass lines slide downward in a series of five semitones. The chaconne is repeated thirteen times. Is it coincidental that that was the number of people present at the Last Supper? There is a real surprise at the end, when after such insistence on the tonality of the chaconne (E minor), after twelve identical E minor cadences, the peaceful final cadence is in the relative major key of G (the key of the "Et in unum"). In part, Bach may have been concerned about the transition to the next movement, which has to be in D major, in order for the trumpets of the resurrection to sound.

Et resurrexit

Which they do. The dead arise, in triumphant fashion.

Et in Spiritum Sanctum

This aria for bass, in duple compound time (6/8), strikes one as both priestly and at the same time dancelike. The pulse is two-to-a-measure, at a slow, processional walk, and yet there is to each pulse an underlying three, like a slow jig. Adding to the dancelike nature of the movement is its orchestration—continuo and two oboes d'amore. The text is quite lengthy and deals with somewhat abstract notions, relatively speaking, such as "one holy catholic and apostolic church"—fundamental to Christian belief, yet not concretely human, unlike its opposite number in the Credo's structure, the soprano and alto duet "Et in unum." At the risk of overstressing this point, do note the relationship in key structure between the two arias. Each is a fifth away from D major, yet in opposite directions—this aria going to the brighter, sharper key. We must be aware of these matters of tonality; because we are soaked in equal temperament, we simply do not hear key differences in the way that Bach's audience would have.

Confiteor

Though unsensational, the Confiteor contains some of the most complex and quietly startling material in the whole Mass. Still in the same general A major tonality, but this time in the relative minor of F-sharp minor (one we have not encountered before, except in passing), the Confiteor is a five-voice fugue accompanied by continuo alone. When in the next movement (Et expecto resurrectionem mortuorum) we return to D major, it will be with trumpets and drums. For now, treating the subjects of baptism and the resurrection of the dead, we are closer to the territory of the opening movement of the Credo, and the musical ideas employ plainchant also. There is a moment when the basses sing the sacramental chant "Confiteor unum baptisma," followed in a canon at the fifth by the altos, then shortly afterward the tenor takes the chant alone, and at half speed, as a cantus firmus and sings the whole chant over an astonishing twenty-six measures while the other voices weave a complex fugue around and above. And it is fitting that it should be the tenors who do this; the word *tenor* originally referred to the singers in an ensemble who held on, tenaciously, as it were, to the cantus firmus while other voices discoursed elaborately around it.

Further surprises await: there is a remarkable adagio section (unusually for Bach, marked as such), to the words "Et expecto resurrectionem mortuorum," which contains chromatic harmonic shifts one would not have thought Bach had in his tonal palette, yet there they are. At one point he has the sopranos sing the same note in each of two measures, the first a C, as the fifth note of the scale of F major, then the exact same sound as a B-sharp, the leading note of the key of C-sharp minor—an otherworldly transformation with which to depict the anticipation of resurrection of the dead. The whole passage of nine measures, by means of which Bach gets us back to D major and the trumpets of the resurrection, is worth careful study.

Et expecto

Bach has actually anticipated the text of this movement in the passage just referred to. For the end of the Credo, Bach reworks material from yet another of his election cantatas, this time the second movement of BWV 120, written for Election Day 1727 in Leipzig. The source material is a massive chorus (about six minutes long). By comparison, the Et expecto scurries by in about two minutes, ending in a glorious *Amen* sung in rapid scuttlings of eighth-notes, which if taken at the appropriate tempo are at the outer border of what is singable.

IV. Sanctus

The Sanctus was originally written for Christmas Day 1724 and is remarkable in calling for a six-part choir. Now, in addition to two soprano lines, the altos are also divided. The text calls for the three-fold repetition of the word *Sanctus,* and this we get in the basses, with three stately downward octave skips, while altos 2 and tenors, then a trio of altos 2 and sopranos 1 and 2 weave upward in triplets, essentially turning what is marked in common time (4/4) into 12/8. Meanwhile, the timpanist starts out with a drum tattoo, which repeats twenty-one times, more than enough to earn the beer of which percussionists are notoriously fond. After their three initial proclamations, the basses start out on a downward phrase consisting of several octave drops, chaconne-like, a pattern repeated in several forms throughout. A bouncy "Pleni sunt coeli," fugal, in quick triple time (3/8), follows, with running passages in sixteenth-notes. Full, indeed, as the Latin word *pleni* ("full") implies.

V. Osanna, Benedictus, Agnus Dei, Dona nobis pacem

Osanna

Fuller yet is the Osanna, which calls for an eight-part or double choir, resulting in quite complex interweavings. This hymn of praise, in D major, of course, is accompanied by chattering alternating subchoirs of flutes 1 and 2, oboes 1 and 2, violins 1 and 2, and trumpets 1, 2, and 3—with ample commentary from the drums, of course.

Benedictus

It seems some time since we were in the key of B minor, and it is a while since we had an aria. The Benedictus is an aria for tenor with flute obbligato (though some think it was intended for violin). The aria opens with a long instrumental introduction, before we hear from the soloist, whose vocal line is slow, passionate, and extremely demanding. The vocal line lies extremely high, even allowing for the pitch at which the mass was likely sung—about one semitone lower than modern concert pitch (A = 415, rather than A = 440). As called for in the liturgy, the Osanna is repeated after the aria.

Agnus Dei

The Agnus Dei is also an aria with obbligato, this time for alto and violins 1 and 2 (not a solo obbligato, therefore). The violin writing is quite low in pitch, occupying about the same range as the solo alto. This slow and rich aria, with wide skips in the vocal line, is one of the favorites of the alto repertoire. One of the best recordings of this aria is by the late English countertenor Alfred Deller. Curiously, the Agnus Dei is in G minor, a key not yet encountered in the Mass, and bearing no relationship to the Osanna that precedes it, and none to the final fugue, Dona nobis pacem.

Dona nobis pacem

This four-voice chorus reprises the music of the Gratias agimus from the Gloria.

Other Works
Motets, *Ascension Oratorio,*
Magnificat, Christmas Oratorio

Motets

As I said at starting, the BWV numbers of Bach's choral music take one into the five hundreds. Besides the Mass in B Minor, the two passions, and the two hundred or so cantatas, there are other works, some very popular, and others less well known.

There are six motets, and a section of BWV 118 often classified as a motet. It would be difficult to define *motet*; it is somewhere between a cantata and an oratorio. Bach's BWV 225, *Singet dem Herrn ein neues Lied* (Sing to the Lord a New Song), is for eight-voice chorus and a large orchestra.

BWV 226, *Der Geist hilft unser Schwachheit auf* (The Spirit Helps Us in Our Frailty), is for eight vocal parts and instruments. It was written for a funeral and is rarely heard.

BWV 227, *Jesu, meine Freude* (Jesu, My Joy), for five voices and continuo, also was perhaps written for a funeral. It is the longest motet, at about twenty minutes. It calls for very talented singers; there is nowhere to hide. It is sometimes performed.

Also perhaps intended as funeral music, BWV 228, *Fürchte dich nicht* (Fear Not), is for eight voices and is sometimes is performed by soloists. It is very difficult.

BWV 229, *Komm, Jesu, komm* (Come, Jesus, Come), is for eight a cappella voices and is also very tricky to sing.

BWV 230, *Lobet den Herrn, alle Heiden* (Praise the Lord, All You Heathen), is sometimes heard. It is for four voice parts and continuo.

Ambitious choirs will sometimes take on a Bach motet. It would be fair to say, I think, that they hold more for the performer than they do for the listener.

BWV 11, *Ascension Oratorio*

Lobet Gott in seinen Reichen (Praise God in His Kingdom) is really a cantata but is sometimes known as the *Ascension Oratorio*. It deserves to be better known. It consists largely of parodies of earlier works by Bach, and one number reappeared as the Agnus Dei of the B Minor Mass. This cantata is intermediate between cantata and oratorio, with tenor Evangelist. The opening chorus has wonderful trumpet and drum fanfares.

BWV 243, *Magnificat*

The *Magnificat* (BWV 243) is frequently performed today. It was premiered on Christmas Eve 1723 and originally was given alongside BWV 63, *Christen, ätzet diesen Tag*, a fairly hefty work in its own right, with drums, trumpets, and everything else one associates with Christmas. In consequence, Bach appears to have decided to keep the *Magnificat* short. This brevity puts it within the reach of any community or church ensemble and makes it something readers would likely enjoy participating in. Here, as an invitation to the reader to get involved, is the opening chorus, which takes less than three minutes to perform.

Chorus, "Magnificat anima mea Dominum" (My Soul Doth Magnify the Lord) (CD Track 18)

Magnificat anima mea Dominum.   My soul doth magnify the Lord.

The key is of course D major! An earlier version was in E-flat, but D is better for trumpets. We are in triple time, but the pulse in really one-in-a-bar. The timpani leave us in no doubt of this. There is no need for subtlety here; one hearty whack a measure will do, and is in fact necessary, for without it, holding on to the detail and the tempo would be difficult. One of the purposes of the continuo is to hold everyone together, and there is so much going on in this texture that without a hearty whack from the timpani at regular intervals, everything could fall apart. The opening ritornello is about a minute long, and the chorus has some catching up to do. The trick for the singers is to keep control of the sixteenth-note turns and runs, while keeping it all light. They sing for less than one minute and twenty seconds in total. There is a fugal section from 1:35 to 1:52, but mostly the chorus is a cheerful and rather light flurry. The Bach Collegium Japan performance is marvelous. Readers interested in the challenges presented by music like this could listen to the recording while using a metronome (the sort that allows you to key in the beats and have the device read out the metronome marking). You will find that even in such a seemingly straight-ahead piece as this, considerable variation in tempo is necessary. The tempi range from 94 to 100, in the course of about two minutes.

There is something for everyone in the *Magnificat*. The arias are all dramatic and short. That said, the forces it calls for are ambitious; it has a five-part chorus (two soprano lines), and Bach asks for five vocal soloists, as well. The orchestra is large, with three trumpets, drums, two flutes, two oboes, two oboes d'amore, strings, and continuo. Particularly exciting for the chorus, besides no. 1 (already discussed), are the last two numbers. Number 12, "Sicut locutus est" (As It Was Spoken to Our Forefathers), is a steady fugue, clear in texture, to be accompanied by continuo only. This gives way to a "Gloria Patri" in French overture format, with a slow section in which the voices spiral upward and downward in triplet figures, to be joined by glorious trumpet fanfares, followed by a trumpet chorus in triple time, reminiscent of the opening chorus.

BWV 248, *Christmas Oratorio*

The *Christmas Oratorio* is a very late work (1734–35) and employs a lot of parody. It is in fact a series of cantatas, intended for performance over a series of Sunday services. In the first performance, BWV 248/1 through 3 were given on December 25, 26, and 27, 1734, with BWV 248/4 through 6 given on January 1, 2, and 6 of 1735. It is sometimes now performed as whole, but it lacks the dynamism of the Mass in B Minor or the passions; it feels like a string of cantatas strung together, which it is. That said, it has some marvelous moments and definitely is something one stands a chance of getting involved in. The first three cantatas would make a great group for performing. Cantatas BWV 248/1 and 3 are in the trumpet key of D major; the second cantata is in G major and is pastoral in feel. There are no trumpets. The opening sinfonia is a pastorale, in compound triple time, with oboe obbligatos. It makes an interesting parallel with Handel's pastoral music in the *Messiah*.

As a *bonne bouche* of farewell to the reader, and an assurance of what pleasures await the interested amateur, here is one of the great chorales from the *Christmas Oratorio*, "Ach mein herzliebes Jesulein" (Ah, My Beloved Jesus-Child). I will make no comment, save to say that the reader by now knows what to listen for.

Chorale, "Ach mein herzliebes Jesulein" (Ah, My Beloved Jesus-Child) (CD Track 19)

Ach mein herzliebes Jesulein,	Ah, my beloved Jesus-child,
Mach dir ein rein sanft Bettelein,	Make for yourself a clean, soft bed
Zu ruhn in meines Herzens Schrein,	Within the temple of my heart,
Dass ich nimmer vergesse dein!	So that I will never forget that I am yours!

Further Reading

Several Web sites are worth exploring—beginning with http://www.bach-cantatas.com. This site will take you everywhere else you might wish to go. It publishes a nationwide compilation of forthcoming performance of the cantatas, and readers who wish to look at scores of the cantatas can find them on the site's page http://www.bach-cantatas.com/IndexScores.htm. The site also has links to "short" scores (containing all the vocal parts, with the orchestral accompaniments presented in a piano reduction).

The *Neue Bach-Ausgabe* (NBA) scores themselves are not downloadable, but the catalog is. See: http://www.bachcentral.com/BachCentral/acrobat/acrobat.html.

For further details on Emmanuel Music, where Bach's cantatas are performed in the U.S. city of Boston, go to http://www.emmanuelmusic.org. Details on the Bach Vespers Choir and Orchestra at Holy Trinity Lutheran church in New York can be found at http://www.bachvespersnyc.org.

Some books I have found useful are as follows:

Bach, Johann Sebastian. *Neue Bach-Ausgabe sämtlicher Werke*. 1954–. (NBA)

Badura-Skoda, Paul. *Interpreting Bach at the Keyboard*. 1995.

David, Hans T., and Arthur Mendel, eds. *The New Bach Reader: A Life of Johann Sebastian Bach in Letters and Documents*. 1966. Revised and expanded by Christoph Wolff, 1998. (NBR)

Day, James. *The Literary Background to Bach's Cantatas*. 1961.

Harnoncourt, Nikolaus. *The Musical Dialogue: Thoughts on Monteverdi, Bach and Mozart*. 2003.

Mellers, Wilfrid. *Bach and the Dance of God*. 1981.

Schweitzer, Albert. *J. S. Bach*. 1911.

Spitta, Philipp. *Johann Sebastian Bach: His Work and Influence on the Music of Germany, 1685–1750.* 1847.
Terry, Charles Sanford. *Bach: The Passions.* 1926.
Wolff, Christoph. *Bach: Essays on His Life and Music.* 1996.
Wolff, Christoph. *Bach: The Learned Musician.* 2000.

Glossary

This glossary should be of interest to anyone who likes to listen to classical music. However, it deals with terms and ideas that are of particular relevance to baroque music in general and to Bach's choral music in particular.

a battuta	In strict tempo, like a clock ticking.
a cappella	Sung without instrumental accompaniment. The underlying meaning is "in the church style."
accidental	Refers to a temporarily altered pitch. For example, in the key of C, which has no flats or sharps, a composer may specify F-sharp.
adagio	Slow tempo.
alla breve	See *cut time.*
allegro	Moderately fast tempo. Remember that Bach himself almost never gave tempo indications, relying on the good judgment of the performer to get the tempo right. There is a clear modern taste for making Bach sound like a sewing machine. Glenn Gould, whose tempos were too often characterized by a helter-skelter gracelessness passing for genius, started this trend, and we are still recovering. Bach must always be gracious.
allemande	A stately and slow baroque dance, the most dignified one of all.

andante   A steady walking tempo, neither too slow nor too
                     quick. Bach would probably have used the term
                     tempo ordinario—normal speed.

antiphonal   Music coming from alternating sides (two choirs, for
                     example, or two different instrumental groups. The
                     St. Matthew Passion, for example, with two SATB
                     choirs and several assorted instrumental groups, is
                     full of antiphonal music.

aria   *Aria* is Italian for "song." In Bach's choral music
                     the arias are self-contained songs (usually for one
                     singer, though there are duets that are really also
                     arias) accompanied by basso continuo and one or
                     some orchestral instruments. The text of an aria
                     will often be commenting on the action or theme
                     in a cantata or oratorio. It will frequently involve
                     the repetition, numerous times, of portions of
                     text. The instrumental accompaniment will often
                     employ an *obbligato* instrument—meaning that
                     the player has to play what is written, rather than
                     improvise. Many of Bach's arias, and other late
                     baroque ones, are *da capo* arias.

arioso   Is intermediate between *recitative* and *aria*. It
                     is more musically elaborate, more melodic than
                     recitative, but like recitative, and unlike aria, the
                     text is stated only once. However, like aria, but
                     unlike recitative, the singer in ariosos usually has
                     more instrumental support. This is often of the-
                     matic importance. In the recits of the *St. Matthew
                     Passion*, Jesus's words are usually sung in arioso
                     and are always accompanied by strings. A striking
                     example of this is given on our CD (Track 14). Bach
                     is depicting the Last Supper (the evening before
                     Jesus's betrayal by Judas, which sets the crucifix-
                     ion narrative in train), when Jesus instituted the

Eucharist (the commemoration of Jesus's life, suffering, and death in the symbolic consumption of bread and wine).

arpeggio   From the Italian for "harp," this means a "broken" chord, in which the notes are played one after another, rather than together.

baroque   The word *baroque* originally described excessive ornamentation in architecture and art and was initially somewhat disapproving. It is now used to refer to a period of artistic and particularly musical history from about 1600 to about 1750. Some subdivide the period and speak of Bach's era as the late baroque.

baroque dance Bach was very fond of dance; there are many types of dance in his instrumental music, and one may enjoy them in the keyboard English suites, French suites, and partitas, as well as in the orchestral suites and in various suites for violin, cello, and flute. But dances are found throughout his choral music, also. Some of his favorite dances were the allemande, courante, minuet, gavotte, and gigue. He was especially fond of this last type, and one of the most remarkable gigues is his gigue fugue for organ, BWV 577.

basso continuo See *continuo.*

brass   In an orchestra, instruments such as trumpets, horns, trombones.

cadence   The etymology of *cadence* means "falling" and describes a moment in music that gives the sense of having come to rest, such as at the end of a piece of music, or of a section, or even merely a phrase. It is achieved through harmony as well as phrasing. In Bach, the resting is often momentary—he comes to a resting point only to pick up the pace again. A particularly definitive form of cadence is the perfect cadence, consisting of chord V followed by chord I in the key one is arriving at. In the key of C, this would be a chord of G followed by a chord of C (that is, the dominant chord followed by the tonic chord). In Bach's recitatives, the end of a narrative phrase is almost always marked by a perfect cadence. There are other kinds of cadence, including the plagal cadence (IV to I) and the interrupted cadence (V to VI). Readers are invited to pick all these out on a keyboard. See also *triad*.

canon   In a canon, one voice (vocal or instrumental) is followed by another, which repeats what the first voice sang while the first voice moves on to new material, which the second voice then also follows. "Row, row, row your boat" is many people's introduction to polyphonic music.

cantata   The basic meaning of the word *cantata*, simply enough, is "something sung." It is of Italian origin and came into use in the sixteenth century. The singers are usually accompanied by instruments, and always so in the case of Bach. Bach did write a set of unaccompanied (*a cappella*) cantata-like pieces, which he termed *motets*. BWV 225 (*Singet dem Herrn ein neues Lied*) and BWV 226 (*Jesu, meine Freude*) are well-known examples of these. Bach's cantatas almost always have several separate movements, some for chorus, some for solo singers.

cantor   In Bach's Lutheran church, a position that carried with it responsibility for music. It was a rather less senior position than Kappellmeister.

cantus firmus In medieval music (when *polyphony* came into being), one line or voice of the music might consist of a chant, or even a popular song, slowed down, sometimes to so snail-like a pace as to be unrecognizable, often sung by the tenor line (so called because it was the tenor's responsibility to hold on to this melody with due tenacity). This came to be called the *cantus firmus*, or foundation melody. Meanwhile, the other musical lines would weave floridly around it. A wonderful example of this practice is the sixteenth-century *Western Wynde Mass* by John Taverner. Contemporary listeners who recognized the cantus firmus would likely have been charmed, or horrified, to recollect the original words of the song: "O western wind, when wilt thou blow, that the small rain down can rain? Christ, if my love were in my arms, and I in my bed again." Bach frequently used the rather more sober Lutheran chorales as cantus firmus melodies in the cantatas and passions. The most famous instance of this is in the opening chorus of the *St. Matthew Passion*, where a choir of boys' voices sings, "O Lamm Gottes unschuldig" (O lamb of God unspotted), slowly, against the elaborate fugal weavings of an eight-part choir. Another example of the cantus firmus is given in the first track on our CD, the opening chorus of BWV 1.

cello piccolo   A small cello, oftentimes one provided with a fifth string, tuned to middle E.

chaconne   A composition with a recurring bass line, sometimes known as a *ground bass*. Bach wrote a famous chaconne for violin.

chorale   A hymn in the Lutheran Church. Chorales tend to have simple and singable tunes, because they were originally intended to be sung by the congregation rather than the choir. They generally have rhyming words and are in a stanzaic form (with the same melody repeating). Martin Luther insisted that worship should be conducted in German, not Latin. He saw that there was a need for such songs in German and wrote many himself. He composed some chorale melodies, including "Ein' feste Burg ist unser Gott" (A Mighty Fortress Is Our God). He sometimes used the old Catholic Gregorian chant melodies and gave them new words in German. "Christ lag in Todesbanden" (Christ Lay in the Bands of Death), on which the cantata BWV 4 is based, is such a chorale.

chorale fantasia   A composition usually having a cantus firmus chorale, with more elaborate accompanying lines. The opening chorus of the *St. Matthew Passion* is a chorale fantasia.

chorale prelude   Chorale tunes also appear in chorale preludes, pieces generally for organ designed to be played immediately before the chorale in worship. Some chorale preludes, or chorale fantasias, may be found in the cantatas. The famous "Jesu, Joy of Man's Desiring," from BWV 147, is a good example of this. It features the chorale in four voices, with added counterpoint.

chord   A group of notes, sounded together, typically consisting of a root note, its third, and its fifth. See *triad*. Also see *cadence*.

chorus   A group of vocal lines, singing together (typically, soprano, alto, tenor, bass).

chorus, double   An eight-voice choir, sometimes divided into two *antiphonal* choirs. In the passions, Bach often used a double choir for dramatic purposes. The opening chorus of the *St. Matthew Passion* is a fine example.

chromatic   Means "colorful." This refers to music that has lots of *accidentals* and changes of harmony and key.

coda	The concluding section of a movement or single composition that usually dwells the work's principal themes and circles around the home key but rarely introduces new material. There is a sense of coming home.
compound time	As opposed to simple measure or rhythm, compound measure has a number of beats that can be subdivided into smaller groups. For example, 12/8 time consists of twelve eighth-notes that group into four sets of three (or one might see it as three groups of four); 6/4 would be two groups of three quarter-notes.
concertino	Played by solo instruments. Its antonym is *ripieno*.
continuo	The continuo is what keeps baroque music ticking. The continuo team in a baroque ensemble usually comprises one or more bass instruments and a harmony instrument. The bass instrument is often a cello or viola da gamba, but it can be a lute, a bassoon, a trombone, or combinations of these, or anything else that makes a low sound. The harmony instrument (which "realizes," or fills out harmonically, the bass line) may be a harpsichord or an organ. The convention nowadays is to have the continuo provided by a cello and harpsichord, but this is based largely on the stated preference of Carl Phillip Emmanuel Bach (one of Bach's many musically talented children).
contrapuntal	The adjective from *counterpoint*.
counterpoint	Two or more different melodies happening at the same time. When this happens, the voices create harmony. The word means, literally, "one note" (*point*) sounding against (*counter*) another.
countersubject	In a fugue, when a voice is done with stating the theme and hands it over to the next voice, the

contrapuntal melody with which the first voice accompanies the second is called the *countersubject*—something that is placed against (*counter*) the subject.

countertenor   A male alto voice.

cut time   A time signature indicating two half-notes per bar (2/2), as opposed to common time, or four quarter-notes per bar (4/4). The distinction between cut and common time lies in the beat — that is, whether there are two beats to a bar or four. Music played in cut time (or "alla breve") should be performed with an underlying two-pulse, and conductors will give the beat accordingly. While common time may be indicated with a symbol resembling a capital "C," cut time would use the same symbol, but with a vertical line going through it.

da capo aria   An aria in three sections. We call the first section A, and the second section B. For the third section we hear A again. It is recapitulated, or taken again from the top. (See *recapitulation*.) *Da capo* means "from the top" and is usually written with the words "al fine," meaning until the stop sign, which is placed just before the B or middle section begins. The recapitulation of the A section may be an ornamented version of its first statement—either written out by the composer or improvised by the performer (sometimes tastelessly so, unfortunately).

dominant   The dominant is the fifth note up from the home tone (or tonic) of a scale. So the dominant note of C is G. And the dominant key of C major is G major. Going the other way, five notes down from C is F. This note is the subdominant. There is no closer relationship (except for the octave) than that between the tonic and its dominant or subdominant. Do note that the tonic is the dominant of its subdominant, and the tonic is the subdominant of its dominant. It all depends how you look at it. Just find these notes on a piano and everything will be clear. Even better, you could find the notes on a guitar and measure the string lengths that correspond to the different notes. If you halve the length of the string, the resulting note will be one octave higher than the original. If you measure off one third of the string, you will find the fifth, or dominant.

dotted rhythm   A dot placed just after a note increases the length of that note. By how much, is the question. By the time of Mozart and Haydn, the answer was by a half. In a pair of notes (termed *dotted notes*), the rhythm is uneven. In baroque music, so-called dotted rhythm was very uneven indeed. Musicologists fight about this matter quite a lot.

eighth-note   See *note duration*.

ensemble   Means "together." It refers to a group of performers.

episode   In a fugue, an episode is a freer moment occurring between the more formal sets of fugal entries.

evangelist   The Evangelist is the storyteller in the *St. John Passion* and the *St. Matthew Passion*. He tells the story in a series of narratives called *recitatives*, in the company of other singers who play Jesus, Peter, Pilate, Judas, and others.

fermata   A pause.

first inversion   See *inversion (chord)*. Also see *root position*.

French overture   An overture in two sections, the first slow and dignified, often with dotted rhythms, the second one fast.

fugal	The adjective from *fugue*.
fugue	A *contrapuntal* composition in which a theme (also known as a "subject") is stated by one "voice" (singer or instrument) and then taken up consecutively by one or more other voices. Meanwhile, voices that have had the theme continue with an accompanying melody called the *countersubject*. Most choral fugues have three or four voices. Bach, the fugue virtuoso par excellence, will turn the theme upside down (inversion), stretch it out to twice its length (augmentation), double it in speed (diminution), have the voices tread on each other's tails (stretto), and often do some or all of these things together. These compositional miracles can be seen and heard in his famous keyboard work *The Well-Tempered Clavier*, forty-eight preludes and fugues, two in each of the major and minor keys, and in *The Art of the Fugue*, written at the end of Bach's life in response to a challenge that he was losing his grip.
gavotte	A baroque dance in four-time, danced at a graceful fast walk.
gigue	A spritely, skipping dance in compound time (6/8, 9/8, or 12/8). Bach loved gigues, and he wrote them all the time. Every suite and partita ends with a gigue, and he wrote many gigue-like movements in the cantatas and oratorios.
half-note	See *note duration*.
harmony	The use of different pitches together, making chords (or discords). *Harmony* often implies nice-sounding, as opposed to *discord*, which means sour-sounding.
hemiola	A rhythmic device in which three groups of two notes alternate with or are played off against two groups of three notes. In his use of the hemiola,

	Bach is exploiting some of the potential of *compound rhythm*.
homophonic	The opposite of *polyphonic*; everyone either singing the same melody (in *unison*) or singing in chords at the same time. Bach's chorales are basically homophonic, though being by Bach they always have some melodic weaving going on among the chords.
interval	The gap between notes. You count both lowest and highest notes. Thus, C to G is a fifth (C, D, E, F, G). D to B is a sixth (D, E, F, G, A, B). C to the C above—eight steps—is an octave.
inversion (chord)	In an inversion, the lowest note may be the third in a triad. In which case the chord is a first inversion, or the fifth, which would make it a second inversion.
inversion (fugue)	In a fugue, the subject is sometimes turned upside down, or inverted.
key	Refers to the harmonic center of a piece of music—the first note (or tonic) of the scale in which a piece is written. We talk of a piece of music as being "in the key of . . . " The Great Mass is in B minor. The opening movement of the *Magnificat* is in D major.
leading note	See *triad*.
librettist	The author of a libretto.
libretto	The text of an oratorio or cantata.
liturgy	Formal public worship or ritual.
Lutheran Church	Lutheranism is the branch of Christianity associated with the teachings of the sixteenth-century German reformer Martin Luther. Luther reformed the practice of the Christianity by challenging the power and authority of the Roman Catholic Church. He launched the Protestant Reformation,

which left Western Christianity divided, as it still is.

major	In a major key, the third is four semitones above the root. It sounds a little more cheerful, a little brighter, than a minor key.
manual	A keyboard on a harpsichord or organ. Many harpsichords have two manuals. Some organs have five manuals.
mediant	See *triad*.
melody	A tune.
menuet	See *minuet*.
minor	In a minor key, the third is three semitones above the root. Minor keys are sadder, or more serious, or more melancholy, than major keys.
minuet	(Or *menuet*.) A baroque dance in triple time, danced at walking pace, therefore a little quicker than the sarabande.
modulation	The movement from one key to another.
motet	A choral composition. It is unclear whether the word refers to the movement of voices against each other or to the presence of a text (*motet* is from the French word for "word").
motive, motif	A short melodic fragment that becomes a building block of more elaborate structures.
note duration	Is measured by a system of division. Starting from a whole-note (white, no tail), a half-note is half the length (white, with a tail). A quarter-note is black, with a tail; an eighth is black, with a tail and a flag or beam; a sixteenth is like the eighth but with two beams; and a thirty-second has three beams. And so on. There are further complications, of course.

Keep separate in your mind eighth (note) and eighth (or octave, the interval). See also *dotted rhythm*.

obbligato An instrumental line in an aria that is obligatory, that cannot be omitted. On our CD Track 4, the Alleluia from cantata 51 has a trumpet obbligato, and CD Track 15, an aria from the *St. Matthew Passion*, has a violin obbligato.

oboe da caccia An oboe pitched a fifth below today's oboe, curved, with a brass bell.

oboe d'amore An oboe that is a little larger, and less assertive in tone, than the modern oboe. It is pitched three semitones below the modern instrument and is sometimes viewed as a transposing instrument. That is, written middle C sounds as the A below.

octave The interval of one eighth, up or down, from a given note. On a keyboard, the octave is about the distance from pinkie to thumb.

parody Borrowed music. Bach frequently borrowed from himself, reusing earlier pieces for later, often rather grand, purposes. The B Minor Mass is full of such parodies.

partita A suite of pieces, in Bach always dance pieces.

passion The story of the suffering and death of Christ, told in each of the first four books of New Testament, was customarily sung during the *liturgy* of Holy Week (commemorating the events beginning with the Last Supper and the subsequent betrayal of Jesus by Judas, through the Crucifixion of Jesus, and culminating in the resurrection of Jesus and the discovery of the empty tomb on what we now term Easter Sunday. In ancient times the story would be sung to plainchant, by an *evangelist*, with other singers taking part in the drama. In time, the crowd took a role also. The sung passion was a precursor of the opera and oratorio. The best-known settings of the passion are those of Bach, most famously the *St. Matthew* and *St. John* passions.

pedal point   A single note, repeated or held, while other voices change the harmony around it. More often than not, pedal points occur in the bass (the term comes from the pedal keyboard of the organ, which sounds the lowest notes). They can occur in other voices, also, and are sometimes called *inverted pedal points*.

perfect cadence   See *cadence*.

piano; pianissimo   Soft; very soft.

pitch, baroque   Pitch has floated up and down over the years. There was no consensus in the eighteenth century, with pitch varying widely. The modern conception of baroque pitch is A at 415 cycles per second. See *pitch, concert*.

pitch, concert   Tuning based on the note A at 440 cycles per second (usually). See *pitch, baroque*.

pizzicato   In stringed instruments, pizzicato notes are plucked with the fingers rather than bowed. Bach was quite fond of pizzicato. Sometimes he has a cello play pizzicato, making it sound quite like a lute.

polyphonic   The opposite of *homophonic*. Polyphonic music (polyphony) has more than one voice (instrumental or vocal), weaving melody together. Fugues are polyphonic. Indeed, almost everything Bach wrote is polyphonic.

prelude   An introductory musical passage.

recapitulation   Coming back to the original theme. In a *da capo aria*, structured ABA, the second A section is the recapitulation.

recitative	The telling of a story (see *evangelist*). In a recitative we hear only one singer at a time; there is no repeating of the text over and over as in an aria, and the accompaniment is normally provided by a bass instrument (cello, viola da gamba, for example) and a harmony instrument, either organ or harpsichord.
ripieno	Full orchestra (the opposite of *concertino*).
ritardando	Slowing down.
ritornello	An instrumental passage that returns in a movement. In many pieces of choral music by Bach we have ritornellos—passages that open the piece and come back in the middle or at the end or both.
root position	In a *triad*, the chord is in root position when the root of the chord is the lowest note. Thus a chord of C will have C in the bass, and the other notes, E and G, are above. If the lowest-sounding note of the chord of C is E, then the chord is in its first inversion. If the lowest note is G, then that is a second inversion.
sacred, secular	*Sacred* music is about religious or holy ideas and is often used in liturgy (formal religious occasions such as the Mass in Christianity). *Secular* is the opposite and has to do with everyday, ordinary, nonholy things. Of course, that does not mean that it is *unholy*, though it can be.
sarabande	A slow dance in triple time, with emphasis on beat two (which is sometimes tied to beat three). In the actual dance, there was often a plié (knee bend) on two, or some dragging of the steps. Bach loved the sarabande; every suite and partita has one.
SATB	Soprano, alto, tenor, bass—the usual composition of a four-part choir.

scale	The ladder of tones on which Western music is based. In C, the major-scale notes are the white keys on a piano keyboard, going up from C to the C above. Terms to describe these notes are as follow. The first note is the tonic, the second is the super-tonic, the third is the mediant, the fourth is the subdominant, the fifth is the dominant, the sixth is the submediant, and the seventh is the leading note.
secular	See *sacred, secular.*
segue	Following straight on from what has just happened.
sinfonia	In baroque music, an orchestral piece, usually part of a larger work; an introduction (a prelude), or interlude, or postlude.
sixteenth-note	See *note duration.*
skipwise	In melody, moving from one note to another that is not adjacent, unlike *stepwise.*
sospiri	A sigh, consisting of two adjacent notes slurred together, from the higher to the lower.
staccato	Staccato notes are detached from each other, as opposed to legato notes, which are played or sung more smoothly. In later music, staccato notes are marked with a dot over or under them, and if they are to be extremely detached, a vertical line is used, like an exclamation point without the dot. Bach almost never used these markings. His performers simply knew what to do.
stepwise	In melody, moving from one note to the next, unlike *skipwise.*
subdominant	See *triad.* Also see *dominant.*
subject	The musical idea. In a fugue, the subject is the melody that each voice sings or plays in turn.
submediant	See *triad.*

supertonic	See *triad*.
temperament	A system of tuning. In equal temperament, the gaps in pitch between the twelve semitones of the scale are evened out, so that it is possible to play in any key. Otherwise (if one generates notes by geometry starting from C), the resultant scale will sound sour in keys having more than about three sharps or flats.
tempo	The rate of speed at which a piece of music is played. After Bach's time, a specific tempo was often indicated by the composer, using words such as *grave*, *lento*, *andante*, *allegretto*, *allegro*, *presto* (those terms are in ascending order of speed). Needless to say, these indications caused more arguments than they shed light. The matter was cleared up somewhat when a man called Winkel invented the metronome (a machine for measuring beats per minute). Composers could then specify a rate of beats (e.g., 126 quarter-notes per minute). Now performers could quarrel with the composers rather than with each other.
tempo ordinario	This looks at first like an unhelpful term, but Bach and Handel and their contemporaries knew exactly what they meant by it, even though they meant two completely different things. It meant ordinary tempo, not slow, but certainly not too fast. It was also used to mean four beats in a measure, sometimes called "common time."
tessitura	The general range of a voice (or instrument). More specifically, this term refers to the part of a range where most of the notes lie in a musical work or where the strongest notes are in a given singer's voice. Bach asked the maximum of his singers. The tessitura of the tenor Evangelist role in the passions is very high.

thirty-second note	See *note duration*.
timpani	Kettledrums.
tonic	The first note of a scale.
triad	A chord, consisting of the root note (for which the chord is named), the third above (counting from the root), and the fifth (counting from the root also). The chord of C (in the key of C this is chord I) therefore is made of the notes C, E, and G. That of G (in the key of C this is chord V) is made of G, B, and D. Chord V followed by chord I is known as a "perfect cadence." See also *cadence*.
triplet	Three notes (of equal length) played in the space of two (which would of course be called a "duplet").
triple time	Three beats to a measure. A waltz or menuet would be a good example of triple time. The first beat of any measure is strong. Thus triple time is counted ONE two three ONE two three.
tutti	All together.
unison	Two or more lines singing or playing the same melody (perhaps an octave apart).
violino piccolo	In Bach's time, a violin smaller than usual, thus sounding higher; or one tuned higher than normal (usually three semitones higher); or one missing the lowest string and having a very high string indeed—so instead of having G, D, A, and E strings it might have D, A, E, and B strings. Bach seems to have been very fond of the violino piccolo.
whole-note	See *note duration*.
woodwinds	In an orchestra, the instruments that are blown, excluding the brass instruments, such as trumpets, horns, and trombones.

CD Track Listing

All performances on the enclosed CD feature the Bach Collegium Japan conducted by Masaaki Suzuki.

1. *Wie schön leuchtet der Morgenstern*, BWV 1: Chorale, "Wie bin ich doch so herzlich froh" (1:36)
   Bach Collegium Japan Orchestra and Chorus
   ℗ 2006 BIS Records AB. Courtesy of BIS Records AB.
   From BIS-SACD-1551

2. *Wie schön leuchtet der Morgenstern*, BWV 1: Chorus, "Wie schön leuchtet der Morgenstern" (8:23)
   Bach Collegium Japan Orchestra and Chorus
   ℗ 2006 BIS Records AB. Courtesy of BIS Records AB.
   From BIS-SACD-1551

3. *Ich hatte viel Bekümmernis*, BWV 21: Chorus, "Das Lamm, das erwürget ist" (3:29)
   Bach Collegium Japan Orchestra and Chorus
   ℗ 1998 Grammofon AB BIS. Courtesy of BIS Records AB.
   From BIS-CD-851

4. *Jauchzet Gott in allen Landen*, BWV 51: Aria, "Alleluia" (2:17)
   Carolyn Sampson, soprano; Bach Collegium Japan Orchestra
   ℗ 2004 & 2005 BIS Records AB. Courtesy of BIS Records AB.
   From BIS-SACD 1471

5. *Du Hirte Israel, höre*, BWV 104: Chorus, "Du Hirte Israel, höre" (4:28)

   Bach Collegium Japan Orchestra and Chorus

   Ⓟ 2002 BIS Records AB. Courtesy of BIS Records AB.

   From BIS-CD-1261

6. *Herz und Mund und Tat und Leben*, BWV 147: Chorus, "Herz und Mund und Tat und Leben" (4:17)

   Bach Collegium Japan Orchestra and Chorus

   Ⓟ 2000 Grammofon AB BIS. Courtesy of BIS Records AB.

   From BIS-SACD 1031

7. *Herz und Mund und Tat und Leben*, BWV 147: Chorale fantasia, "Jesus bleibet meine Freude" (3:21)

   Bach Collegium Japan Orchestra and Chorus

   Ⓟ 2000 Grammofon AB BIS. Courtesy of BIS Records AB.

   From BIS-SACD 1031

8. *St. John Passion*, BWV 245: Recitative with choral interjections, "Jesus ging mit seinen Jüngern" (2:25)

   Evangelist: Gerd Türk, tenor; Jesus: Chiyuki Urano, bass; Bach Collegium Japan Orchestra and Chorus

   Ⓟ 1998 & 1999 BIS Records AB. Courtesy of BIS Records AB.

   From BIS-CD-9021-1

9. *St. John Passion*, BWV 245: Recitative with choral interjection, "Und Hannas sandte ihn gebunden" (2:21)

   Evangelist: Gerd Türk, tenor; Peter: Chiyuki Urano, bass; Servant: Makoto Sakurada, tenor; Bach Collegium Japan Orchestra and Chorus

   Ⓟ 1998 & 1999 BIS Records AB. Courtesy of BIS Records AB.

   From BIS-CD-9021-1

10. *St. John Passion*, BWV 245: Aria, "Ach, mein Sinn" (2:36)

Makoto Sakurada, tenor; Bach Collegium Japan Orchestra

Ⓟ 1998 & 1999 BIS Records AB. Courtesy of BIS Records AB.

From BIS-CD-9021-1

11. *St. John Passion*, BWV 245: Aria with choral interjections, "Eilt, ihr angefochtnen Seelen" (4:13)

Peter Kooij, bass; Bach Collegium Japan Orchestra and Chorus

Ⓟ 1998 & 1999 BIS Records AB. Courtesy of BIS Records AB.

From BIS-CD-9021-1

12. *St. John Passion*, BWV 245: Aria, "Es ist vollbracht" (6:09)

Yoshikazu Mera, countertenor; Bach Collegium Japan Orchestra

Ⓟ 1998 & 1999 BIS Records AB. Courtesy of BIS Records AB.

From BIS-CD-9021-2

13. *St. Matthew Passion*, BWV 244: Chorus with chorale cantus firmus, "Kommt, ihr Töchter" (8:07)

Bach Collegium Japan Orchestra and Chorus

Ⓟ 1998 & 1999 BIS Records AB. Courtesy of BIS Records AB.

From BIS-CD-9021-3

14. *St. Matthew Passion*, BWV 244: Recitative, "Er antwortete und sprach" (2:53)

Evangelist: Gerd Türk, tenor; Jesus: Peter Kooij, bass; Judas: Chiyuki Urano, bass; Bach Collegium Japan Orchestra

Ⓟ 1998 & 1999 BIS Records AB. Courtesy of BIS Records AB.

From BIS-CD-9021-3

15. *St. Matthew Passion*, BWV 244: Aria, "Erbarme dich" (6:10)

Robin Blaze, countertenor; Bach Collegium Japan Orchestra

Ⓟ 1998 & 1999 BIS Records AB. Courtesy of BIS Records AB.

From BIS-CD-9021-4

16. Mass in B Minor, BWV 232: Chorus, "Gloria in excelsis Deo" (1:42)

    Bach Collegium Japan Orchestra and Chorus

    ℗ 2007 BIS Records AB. Courtesy of BIS Records AB.

    From BIS-CD-9020-1

17. Mass in B Minor, BWV 232: Chorus, "Et in terra pax" (4:56)

    Bach Collegium Japan Orchestra and Chorus

    ℗ 2007 BIS Records AB. Courtesy of BIS Records AB.

    From BIS-CD-9020-1

18. *Magnificat*, BWV 243: Chorus, "Magnificat anima mea Dominum" (2:52)

    Bach Collegium Japan Orchestra and Chorus

    ℗ 1999 BIS Records AB. Courtesy of BIS Records AB.

    From BIS-CD-1011

19. *Christmas Oratorio*, BWV 248/1: Chorale, "Ach mein herzliebes Jesulein" (1:29)

    Bach Collegium Japan Orchestra and Chorus

    ℗ 1998 & 2005 BIS Records AB. Courtesy of BIS Records AB.

    From BIS-CD-9022-1

UNLOCKING THE MASTERS

The highly acclaimed Unlocking the Masters series brings readers into the world of the greatest composers and their music. All books come with CDs that have tracks taken from the world's foremost libraries of recorded classics, bringing the music to life.

"With infectious enthusiasm and keen insight, the Unlocking the Masters series succeeds in opening our eyes, ears, hearts, and minds to the great composers." – *Strings*

BACH'S CHORAL MUSIC: A LISTENER'S GUIDE
by Gordon Jones
US $22.99 • 978-1-57467-180-3 • HL00332767

BACH'S KEYBOARD MUSIC: A LISTENER'S GUIDE
by Victor Lederer
US $22.99 • 978-1-57467-182-7 • HL00332830

BEETHOVEN'S SYMPHONIES: A GUIDED TOUR
by John Bell Young
US $22.95 • 978-1-57467-169-8 • HL00331951

BRAHMS: A LISTENER'S GUIDE
by John Bell Young
US $22.95 • 978-1-57467-171-1 • HL00331974

CHOPIN: A LISTENER'S GUIDE TO THE MASTER OF THE PIANO
by Victor Lederer
US $22.95 • 978-1-57467-148-3 • HL00331699

DEBUSSY: THE QUIET REVOLUTIONARY
by Victor Lederer
US $22.95 • 978-1-57467-153-7 • HL00331743

DVOŘÁK: ROMANTIC MUSIC'S MOST VERSATILE GENIUS
by David Hurwitz
US $27.95 • 978-1-57467-107-0 • HL00331662

THE GREAT INSTRUMENTAL WORKS
by M. Owen Lee
US $27.95 • 978-1-57467-117-9 • HL00331672

EXPLORING HAYDN: A LISTENER'S GUIDE TO MUSIC'S BOLDEST INNOVATOR
by David Hurwitz
US $27.95 • 978-1-57467-116-2 • HL00331671

LISZT: A LISTENER'S GUIDE
by John Bell Young
US $22.99 • 978-1-57467-170-4 • HL00331952

THE MAHLER SYMPHONIES: AN OWNER'S MANUAL
by David Hurwitz
US $22.95 • 978-1-57467-099-8 • HL00331650

OPERA'S FIRST MASTER: THE MUSICAL DRAMAS OF CLAUDIO MONTEVERDI
by Mark Ringer
US $29.95 • 978-1-57467-110-0 • HL00331665

GETTING THE MOST OUT OF MOZART: THE INSTRUMENTAL WORKS
by David Hurwitz
US $22.95 • 978-1-57467-096-7 • HL00331648

GETTING THE MOST OUT OF MOZART: THE VOCAL WORKS
by David Hurwitz
US $22.95 • 978-1-57467-106-3 • HL00331661

PUCCINI: A LISTENER'S GUIDE
by John Bell Young
US $22.95 • 978-1-57467-172-8 • HL00331975

SCHUBERT: A SURVEY OF HIS SYMPHONIC, PIANO, AND CHAMBER MUSIC
by John Bell Young
US $22.99 • 978-1-57467-177-3 • HL00332766

SCHUBERT'S THEATER OF SONG: A LISTENER'S GUIDE
by Mark Ringer
US $22.99 • 978-1-57467-176-6 • HL00331973

SHOSTAKOVICH SYMPHONIES AND CONCERTOS: AN OWNER'S MANUAL
by David Hurwitz
US $22.95 • 978-1-57467-131-5 • HL00331692

SIBELIUS, THE ORCHESTRAL WORKS: AN OWNER'S MANUAL
by David Hurwitz
US $27.95 • 978-1-57467-149-0 • HL00331735

TCHAIKOVSKY: A LISTENER'S GUIDE
by Daniel Felsenfeld
US $27.95 • 978-1-57467-134-6 • HL00331697

DECODING WAGNER: AN INVITATION TO HIS WORLD OF MUSIC DRAMA
by Thomas May
US $27.95 • 978-1-57467-097-4 • HL00331649

AMADEUS PRESS
www.amadeuspress.com

Prices and availability subject to change without notice.